The Book of the
LORD NELSON 4-6-0s

By Richard Derry

A British Railways Illustrated Special

Acknowledgements

It is getting on for half a century since I last saw a Nelson in everyday BR action; much of the story, as with other classes, can only be pieced together from the work and memories of many others, added to one's own determined footslogging round the libraries, museums and the Record Office. So I'm only too happy, as always, to acknowledge this help and advice. Thanks are due, in especial, to Eric Youldon and to D.W. Winkworth, without whose (respectively) later appraisal and earlier research I don't think the book would have got started. Ian Sixsmith, Chris Hawkins, Martin Smith of *Railway Bylines* magazine, Peter Groom, Hamish Stevenson, R.C. Riley, Gavin Morrison, Ronald Wilkinson, Peter Kemmett, Eddie Scrumpter, Kevin Coventry and Bryan Wilson all gave valuable time and assistance, while my publisher's ministrations at *The Kildare Lodge Hotel*, Minehead and *The Royal Oak*, Winsford helped when the going got tough. Mention must also be made, of course, to the *Howard of Effingham* in Effingham, Surrey. Many of the photographs, again, come from the inestimable Transport Treasury – Gate House, North Road, Insch, Aberdeenshire, AB52 6XP. If you have any negatives give them a call – 01464 820863; *www.transporttreasury.co.uk*

Dedication
This book is for Mick and Dave Smith, my lifelong friends.

First published in the United Kingdom in 2005
by Irwell Press Limited, 59A, High Street, Clophill,
Bedfordshire MK45 4BE
Printed by Newton Printing

Contents

Foreword

I've never calculated the hours spent researching the 'Books Of'; so many arcane, mysterious, near-untranslatable and sometimes contradictory data have swum before my eyes over the years that it would be hard to even guess at now. The Nelsons were a little more awkward than most, for the reference documents were more fragmentary and more widely dispersed. I managed to see the whole class before they were withdrawn; all were at Eastleigh by then and working boat trains such as the Cunarder, or on the Waterloo-Bournemouth trains which in latter days included a 12.22pm Saturday working in summer. It was the preponderance of such trains on the Southern that really, I think, saw the Nelsons last so long. The 12.22pm was memorable as one of the last down trains to see before the rush back home for lunch and more than one Nelson was nabbed on that train. My last one came on a miserable Friday autumn evening in 1961 during a brief visit to our favourite lineside haunt at Weybridge in Surrey. Just one more down train

before the off and it was 30861 LORD ANSON looking very dull and drab as it ran under the road bridge. I'd cleared my Nelsons but the class only had one year to go; now, more than forty years later I reflect, I'm in the Reading Room of the National Archives at Kew piecing together the repair history of the class.

Crucial records used for other Southern classes are not available for the Nelsons, and some works visits have been divined from separate, but again patchy, boiler records, yet it is clear that gaps, particularly in the 1930s and 1940s, exist. It is hoped to render down the boiler data into some further tabulated information for the *Photographic Accompaniment* for the Lord Nelsons.

Lastly, the strange tale of Scamp and LORD ANSON. A collie cross, he belonged to my oldest friends, Mick and Dave Smith and was addicted to chasing bikes, cars, buses, all other dogs and – we discovered – trains. Mick and Dave's Dad Bill was a Guard on the Weybridge-Virginia Water branch, often getting up at 3am to cycle to Chertsey and start

his shift. One day we all went to meet Bill off his early shift, the walk taking us along the path in the local heath that still looks down on the cutting leading to Weybridge station, the eastern approach. Here Scamp took up his usual routine, diving under the wire and chasing the first steam train that came along, rushing back up the embankment to collapse in the nearest puddle with tongue lolling out. Then he was off again, only this time it was LORD ANSON (again) on an up train and we were dumbfounded *as the dog ran under the train.* After a stunned moment, full of the vision of Scamp horribly mangled, the dynamic, if insane, dog appeared on the far side and collapsed in another puddle to reinvigorate himself for the next train. He lived for another six years, still chasing everything in sight, but at a slower pace.

Richard Derry, Minehead, 2005

Nelson transformation. Top, shimmering power with even the buffers burnished as one of the first engines, early on in its career, gets ready at Dover for the next boat train to London. At Basingstoke shed more than thirty years later, on 17 August 1962, 30861 LORD ANSON is a very different figure with all the numerous detail changes. Even the lamp irons are altered, in shape and form. The location is a more profound indication of the changed circumstances of the class; from top notch express to a main line stopper. Behind is a Schools 4-4-0, 30925 CHELTENHAM. Photographs E. Scrumpter Collection, John Scrace.

'EXCELLENT TO A DEGREE'

It was with some trepidation that I approached *The Book of the Lord Nelsons*, for I knew the class little compared with earlier collaborations with Irwell Press, *The Books of* the Britannias, BR Standards and the Bulleid Pacifics. Among the various luminaries to whose corrective rod I must submit in order to put these volumes together it seemed a fairly general feeling that here lay perils abundant for the 'engine picker'. 'No single engine was the same as another' seemed a daunting prospect. No one has helped create this series of books quite like Eric Youldon of Exeter so it was to this student of locomotives that I turned. This is what he wrote:

Thanks for your letter concerning future 'Books of', Nelsons Schools and Arthurs. I am pleased these are going ahead as all three have always been favourites with me. I shall of course be pleased to assist as I have done in the past with similar Irwell volumes. I am not too sure what you have in mind for 'framework of reference' but the main books, purely picture books apart, on these classes to date are:-
a) *Maunsell's Nelsons* by D.W. Winkworth (Allen & Unwin)
b) *The Schools 4-4-0s* by D.W. Winkworth (Allen & Unwin)
c) *Locos of the LSWR* Vol. 2 by D.L. Bradley (RCTS)
d) *Locos of the SR* Vol. I by D.L. Bradley (RCTS)
e) *LSWR Locos, Urie Classes* by D.L. Bradley (Wild Swan)

The first two are especially good, as we expect from D. W .Winkworth.

The yarn about no two Nelsons being the same is slightly over the top; there were certainly some significant features confined to a particular locomotive, but to say every one was different is no more true than could be said about almost any type. If you went over a class of engines that's been in service a number of years, with a strong eye-glass, there's bound to be subtle differences, even if it is only in the way such items as frames and boilers got patched up to suit each case. I would suggest that by the time they were withdrawn there was no significant difference between 30850, 30853, 30854, 30855, 30856, 30857, 30858, 30860, 30861, 30862 and 30864. The 'odd' ones would be:

30851 - non-standard cylinders
30852 - long boiler and modified chimney
30859 - 6ft 3in coupled wheels
30863 - Maunsell pattern cylinders
30865 - 90 degree crank setting
I don't doubt there were other small details that differed, but so there were with all types.
Yours,

In fact, Eric's sensible points are valuable in two ways – they prompted the swift finalising of this book and they remind us that maybe we've overdone this 'engine picking' business just a little. It's interesting and fun, after all, and not a virility test. Certainly I would hate to be a model manufacturer these days, such is the heightened awareness of locomotive detail variation. I've pointed out all the differences I can in the Lord Nelsons, relying heavily on the blessed band who figure in the credits of all these Irwell titles. A great deal of time and sorrow was saved through consulting D.W. Winkworth's aforementioned *Maunsell's Nelsons*; the whole story is laid out to a degree of detail, comprehensiveness and mastery of detail that the rest of us can only gawp at. In past 'Books Of' we have usually uncovered a few nuggets that are wholly new – but only barely so in the case of the Nelsons, I deem. To the details set out in *Maunsell's Nelsons*, as updated here and there in the light of subsequent knowledge by Eric Youldon, this book

LORD NELSON at Dover on one of the jobs the class were to have made their own, a continental boat train. The great part of the class was at Stewarts Lane (or 'Battersea' as it was more commonly known) through the 1930s for this work, forming the 'Continental Link' together with a couple of King Arthurs. In these years they acquired an unfortunate reputation for poor steaming, excessive coal consumption and unpredictable performances. The most damning verdict was an expressed preference for an Arthur on the job. It was a case familiar throughout the story of steam: not enough men getting enough experience of a particular engine type, finding difficulties and rapidly developing an aversion to their charges. Photograph The Transport Treasury.

LORD NELSON at Nine Elms, fitted up with the indicator shelter. This would be its period of evaluation on the Western Section, the old LSW, after running in from Eastleigh and exhibition at various places as 'the most powerful passenger locomotive in the country'. In particular the indicated running was on the sixteen coach Atlantic Coast Express in April 1927, where LORD NELSON easily achieved Maunsell's goal of 1,500HP. The wider goal of '500 tons at 55mph' would seem to be in reach, but it was at the cost of disappointingly high coal consumption. Power class 'A' on running plate behind buffer beam. The linkage from crosshead to indicating equipment can be discerned. Photograph W.G. Boyden courtesy Frank Hornby.

owes much. There are now *Photographic Accompaniments* published or in preparation for all of the 'Book Of' titles, so any details overlooked or clangers committed can always be highlighted later when, as happens with all the previous volumes, readers contact the publisher. *I was puzzled by...* and *I draw your attention to...* they usually begin and I am humbled once again! Oh, and to the book list I'd add *Arthurs, Nelsons and Schools of the Southern*, by S.C. Townroe and *Maunsell Locomotives*, by Brian Haresnape (both Ian Allan).

****

The origins of the Lord Nelsons lay way back in a vanished world when the railways were just about the most glamorous institution we had, along with the Monarchy, the Services, trans-Atlantic liners and so on. The first of this class of large 4-6-0 was but one in a string of new locomotives over the generations that was deliberately presented to catch the public eye. When was the last time a new British locomotive was unveiled on the evening TV for instance?

Civil engineering moulded the development of the Lord Nelson 4-6-0s; R.E.L. Maunsell, in the 1920s, had to find a locomotive design able to run over all the Southern's varied main routes (with axle and loading gauge restrictions like no other) with 500 ton trains at speeds approaching 60mph; '500 tons at 55mph' became the call. Axle load was crucial and the 1920s saw a tension develop between the Civil Engineer and the Locomotive Engineer on British railway companies that was to last decades. Locomotives now had to be designed for ever greater speed and utility, not only within existing height and width constraints but to a strict axle limit. As Townroe puts it, the Lord Nelson design is deserving of a special place in the history of British locomotive development, 'as an exercise in ingenuity to secure a significant increase in power of a 4-6-0 type with a minimal increase in weight'.

The design and development of the Lord Nelsons involved some protracted wrangling between Maunsell and the Civil Engineer and the 'departmental clash' with its volleys of memos and paper skirmishes can be readily imagined. Bradley describes Maunsell amassing a whole store of learned opinion, from other CMEs and private builders, both here and abroad, to wrest an increase in axle limits from the SR Chief Civil Engineer, George Ellson. A limited increase was allowed, apparently, only for a *reduction* to be imposed once the drawings had been laboriously prepared. Maunsell's reaction can only be imagined... The design was finally accepted in June 1925, the axle loading reduced to 21 tons 13 cwt in the time-honoured way, by using lighter steels, cutting holes, reducing thicknesses and so on.

No.E850 LORD NELSON, completed in 1926, saw the process of squeezing more and more power into an existing profile that we see with all the great designs, throughout the history of UK locomotive development. The new giant 4-6-0 superseded the King Arthurs (of which Maunsell built a number at this period, improving the earlier Urie ones and 'plugging the power gap' before the new Lord Nelson was developed) and bore power/weight 'fruit' of a staggering kind. The new Lord Nelson was hardly more than a ton heavier than a Maunsell Arthur yet for a driving axle weight increase of less than half a ton, the Nelson provided an astonishing increase in tractive effort of something like a third, from 25,321lbs to 33,510lbs. In all of this, publicity was a consideration, one that doubtless gave Maunsell allies on the Board in his deliberations with the CCE. It was no accident that LORD NELSON turned out to be 'the most powerful passenger engine in the country...' What follows (page 5) is *The Railway Gazette* account of the new engine's unveiling, a good old-fashioned 'trade' account.

Above. E851 SIR FRANCIS DRAKE, working a boat train. When the Southern was formed it found itself with three groups of locomotives with duplicate numbers, so a simple way of differentiating them was to give SECR locos an A (for Ashford), LBSCR locos a B (for Brighton) and LSWR locos an E, for Eastleigh. So, for example, E470 was a D15 4-4-0, B470 an E4 0-6-2T and A470 a D 4-4-0. New locomotives were given the appropriate letter for their Section, so the Lord Nelsons (though most worked first on the Eastern Section) got E because they were maintained at Eastleigh – hence E850. N 2-6-0s, repaired at Ashford, got an A, as in A850. The letters were abandoned in 1931 with no further change for Western Section engines, so that our E470 example was now simply 470. On the Central Section the B was dropped and 2000 added so that B470 became 2470. Eastern Section locos had 1000 added so that A470 became 1470. There was an exception for the Z class 0-8-0Ts, A950-A957 becoming simply 950-

957. This meant they were now considered to come under the Western Section. That is 'The A, B and E of it' from Mr. Youldon; in my completely at-sea original interpretation (now obviously abandoned) of the 'E' and other prefixes I asked (a foresight was upon me) 'Am I talking rubbish?' 'F'raid so' he replied, hence the gold-plated account above. Photograph The Transport Treasury.

Below. 851 SIR FRANCIS DRAKE in original condition at Stewarts Lane. It's not a look we are used to of course, being so familiar with the smoke deflectors, but in this form the Nelsons certainly had an air of great bulk. Looking at SIR FRANCIS in this brooding mood you'd certainly believe it was one of the 'most powerful passenger locomotives in the country'. Observe early shallow bogie frame; compare, for example, with 30858 LORD DUNCAN at Nine Elms later in this section. Photograph F.H. Stingemore, The Transport Treasury.

Above. 852 SIR WALTER RALEIGH with Lemaître exhaust and high sided tender passing Folkestone (the shed coal stage is on the left). The 'No' on the buffer beam has gone. Photograph The Transport Treasury.

Below. 855 ROBERT BLAKE (again – early bogie frame) at Stewarts Lane. The average cost of the first batch of ten Nelsons, Bradley records, was £10,150, considerably less than the £15,000 plus of LORD NELSON. The latter figure obviously reflected all the 'start up' costs of patterns, jigs, drawings and so on though, to lessen the book price, E850 was looked upon as a substitute for the King Arthur that was cancelled, E807. Photograph F.H. Stingemore, The Transport Treasury.

Pre-war Eastern Section line up at Stewarts Lane. The Nelson on the left is the taper boiler 857 LORD HOWE with the oddly 'cranked' smoke deflectors. SIR BORS DE GANIS stands alongside. Photograph H.N Shepherd, The Transport Treasury.

THE RAILWAY GAZETTE.

OCTOBER 15, 1926.

NEW FOUR-CYLINDER 4-6-0 TYPE EXPRESS LOCOMOTIVE, SOUTHERN RAILWAY.

A Design Incorporating some Distinctive Features.   Adhesion Weight, 62 tons.   Tractive Effort, 33,500 lb.

There was recently completed at the Eastleigh Works of the Southern Railway a new locomotive of the 4-6-0 type with four single-expansion cylinders, designed by Mr R.E.L. Maunsell, the Chief Mechanical Engineer, to meet the requirements of increasingly heavy passenger trains running in accordance with fast schedules. This engine, which is numbered E.850 and bears the name *Lord Nelson*, constitutes the first of the series to be known as the 'Nelson' class, and some distinctive features are incorporated in its design.

In point of tractive power development, the engine marks an advance upon the 'King Arthur' class, and, indeed on this, the commonly accepted basis of power computation for steam locomotives, it ranks as the most powerful passenger engine in Great Britain, the tractive effort, at 85 per cent of the boiler pressure, 220lb per sq in being 14.95 tons (33,500lb).

The inside cylinders are placed slightly in advance of the outside ones, and are formed in one casting with their piston valve steam chests above them. These cylinders drive the crank axle of the foremost pair of coupled wheels, and steam distribution to them is effected by separate inside Walschaerts valve motions actuated by single eccentrics. The outside cylinders are separate castings integral with piston valve steam chests, and these drive the middle pair of coupled wheels, steam distribution in this case being performed by outside Walschaerts gearing having the usual arrangement of return cranks. The steam passages and piping are laid out to advantage in such a way as to secure free circulation of the steam to and from the cylinders.

An interesting feature of the design in this connection is that there are eight separate impulses per revolution of the coupled wheels, this resulting from a special disposition of the crank pins, by means of which the individual exhausts from both ends of all cylinders occur separately instead of the usual arrangement of synchronised exhausts giving four beats per revolution of the wheels in four-cylinder engines having quartered cranks. About two years ago Mr Maunsell experimented with this arrangement of cylinders and cranks by altering one of the late Mr Dugald Drummond's four-cylinder engines. This engine (No.449) as originally arranged had the four cylinders, two inside and two outside the frames, driving on two axles with the cranks quartered and having the usual four impulses per revolution. The alteration made was to turn the cranks of the inside engine through 45 degrees and re-balance the wheels to suit. The improvement secured by this alteration was so remarkable that it was decided to embody the arrangement in the new engines of the 'Nelson' class. The arrangement provides a more uniform torque and also more regular firebox draught than is possible with the customary system. The revolving and reciprocating parts have been made as light as possible by using a special high tensile steel, and the advantage gained thereby is also reflected in the lightness of the balance weights in the wheels.

The boiler is of large proportions, and a new feature for engines built at Eastleigh is the provision of a Belpaire pattern firebox. This latter is of liberal dimensions, with sloping

LORD HOWE in both its guises, at Salisbury. It carried the taper boiler no.1063 (below) for two periods, 1937-1941 and 1943-1945. The idea, it is said, was to gain experience of this sort of boiler as a prelude to the introduction of a Pacific express passenger locomotive and a goods 4-8-0. It had a round top firebox, combustion chamber and 'Sinuflo' superheater rather than Maunsell's design; the reduced height of the chimney and dome (because the boiler was pitched higher) exaggerated the impression of much greater size compared to the conventional Nelsons. The taper boiler had an extended row of washout plugs along the firebox, one of many obvious differences from the rest of the Nelson boilers; this was for the benefit of the combustion chamber. After lingering for several years on the boiler dump at the back of Eastleigh works, boiler no.1063 went for scrap in 1952. Later deep frame bogie clearly shown; these were introduced around the mid-1930s. Photographs The Transport Treasury.

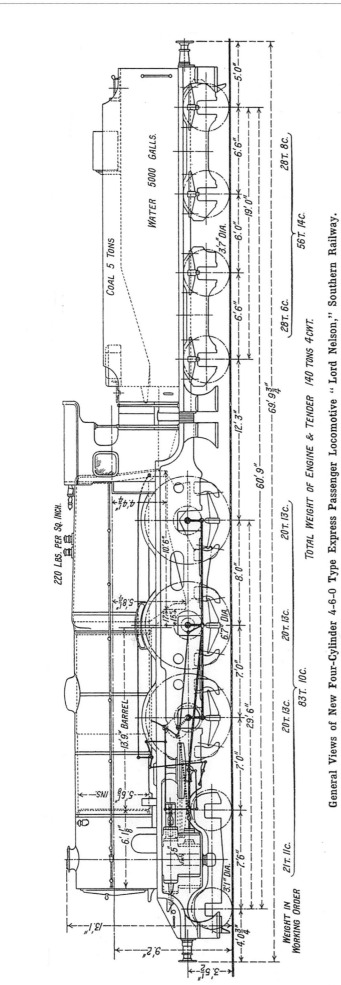

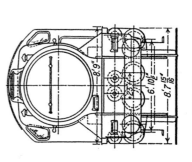

General Views of New Four-Cylinder 4-6-0 Type Express Passenger Locomotive "Lord Nelson," Southern Railway.

Mr. R. E. L. Maunsell, C.B.E., Chief Mechanical Engineer.

End View,
New S.R. Locomotive.

No.858 LORD DUNCAN storms through the Folkestone Warren with an up boat train. With the 'Boat Link' established at Stewarts Lane there was the opportunity to improve the performance of the class and after a while the schedule between *Victoria* and *Dover Marine* was reduced to 95 minutes. This was fairly moderate but even so, many of the performances were uninspiring. D.W. Winkworth in his book *Maunsell's Nelsons* reports sifting through a number of logs which demonstrate late arrivals and inadequate performances. Note 'plain top' chimney. Photograph Dr Ian Allen, The Transport Treasury.

858 LORD DUNCAN, now on the Western Section, at Waterloo in 1939. It had been at Stewarts Lane from new but had gone to Nine Elms at the end of 1938. In part at least, it seems, because the Salisbury men did not take to the class, after a while they were confined to work east of Salisbury. Still sports plain top chimney. Photograph K. Pullen, The Transport Treasury.

roof and backplate. The firebox water space stays are of steel in the fire area with nuts on the fire side and ordinary riveted copper stays elsewhere. The tubes are of moderate length, there being 173 small tubes 2in external diameter and 27 large tubes 5¼in external diameter.

The superheater header is of the 'Maunsell' type, with air-relief valves. Safety valves of the Ross patent 'pop' type are mounted upon the firebox, and the fire door is of the sliding type. Other fittings include a soot blower, exhaust injector, and a 4-feed sight feed lubricator with separate condenser for the cylinders and valve chests. The cab is particularly commodious and the controls well and conveniently arranged.

The engine in working order, without tender, weighs 83 tons 10cwt and of this approximately 62 tons rank as adhesion weight. This, we believe, is the highest figure yet reached both in respect of individual axle loading and collective adhesion weight in a 4-6-0 type of engine, although a 21-ton axle load was employed on the North Eastern Railway some few years back, the engines being of the 4-4-0 type. The weight supported by the leading bogie is 21 tons 11 cwt. This bogie is of simple and robust construction with side-controlled springs, arranged for adjustment and removal, from the outside of the frame, while side steadying bearings to the main frame are provided.

The following are the principal particulars:-

Cylinders (4) diam	16½in
Cylinders piston stroke	26in
Coupled wheels, diam.	6ft 7in
Coupled bogie whls, diam.	3ft 1in
Wheelbase, rigid	15ft 0in
Wheelbase, bogie	7ft 6in
Wheelbase engine, total	9ft 6in
Boiler –	
Height of centre from rail	9ft 2in
Diam inside at front	5ft 6½in
Diam outside at firebox	5ft 9in
Length of barrel	13ft 9in
Length betw'n tube pl'tes	4ft 2in
Firebox, width	4ft 0½in
Firebox, length, inside	10ft 6in
Heating surface –	
Firebox	194 sq ft
Small tubes	1282 sq ft
Large tubes	513 sq ft
Total	1989 sq ft
Superheater surface	376 sq ft
Combined	2365 sq ft
Grate area	33 sq ft
Boiler pressure	220lb sq in
Tractive effort, at 85% boiler pressure	14.95 tons (33,500lb)
Adhesive factor, at 85% boiler pressure	4.1

The tender is of the 8-wheeled double bogie pattern, and has a capacity for 5000 gallons of water and 5 tons of coal. Three steel reservoirs are mounted abreast at the rear end of the tender, these providing enhanced brake power for the wheels of the tender. The barrels are connected directly to the top of the vacuum

brake cylinders by piping. When fully loaded the tender weighs 56 tons 14 cwt, making a total for engine and tender in working order of 140 tons 4 cwt.

In this engine, Mr Maunsell has produced a well-designed and highly-efficient development of the 4-6-0 type in accordance with British practice standards. The appearance of the engine is excellent to a degree, and judging by its performance during the inaugural trip on Tuesday last, October 12, when the engine took the 'Atlantic Coast' express from Waterloo to Salisbury, it has a considerable reserve of power in hand when working trains of between 400 and 450 tons weight. Actually, the engine has been constructed to haul trains of 500 tons at an average speed of 55 miles per hour, the heaviest trains on the Southern Railway at the present time being from 425 to 450 tons.

The overall dimensions of the *Lord Nelson* are such as to enable it to run on any main line of the Southern system. When other engines of the 'Nelson' class are built, they will bear the following names i.e. *Lord St Vincent, Howard of Effingham, Lord Howe, Sir Francis Drake, Lord Rodney, Sir Walter Raleigh, Lord Hood, Sir Richard Grenville, Lord Hawke* and *Martin Frobisher*. The new class in no way renders the 'Kings Arthurs' obsolete. On the contrary, additions are about to be made to this series.

Long boilered E860 LORD HAWKE looking perfect at Nine Elms on 22 March 1930, with Urie 5,000 gallon curved top tender and the lovely, intricate, sage green livery with lining on cylinders, running plate, splashers and so on. They certainly looked the part, even if performances were less than perfect. There was no visible vacuum pump on a Nelson because there was no suitable place to mount it as there was, for example, on a King Arthur. It was therefore located inside the frames and was driven by the inside left-hand crosshead. It can be seen in the frame plan on page 88. Pumps were removed from all SR locos about 1939. A good study of the early bogie. Photograph W.G. Boyden, courtesy Frank Hornby.

E859 LORD HOOD with a boat train and Urie 5,000 gallon curved top tender. The 'boats' at this period often had this curious wagon behind the engine with what looks like chained down containers. Customs sealed perhaps? Photograph F.H. Stingemore, The Transport Treasury.

The instinct for publicity that saw LORD NELSON run out as Britain's 'most powerful passenger locomotive' ensured that maximum coverage went to its first venture in the public eye, on what else but the Atlantic Coast Express, as *The Railway Gazette* notes. What follows below is the contemporary account, based closely on the official press 'handout'. The Inaugural Trip was made on the 11.0am (the ACE) on Tuesday 12 October 1926 from Waterloo to Salisbury and back, a distance of 83 miles 60 chains in either direction. Separate coaches were provided for a number of guests, with a dining car and corridor coach attached at the front for their comfort. Luncheon was served on the outward journey, and tea on the return one, and on arrival at Salisbury the guests were conveyed 'by charabanc to Stonehenge, visiting Salisbury Cathedral on the way back to the station'.

Those representing the Southern Railway were: Mr R.E.L. Maunsell, CBE, Chief Mechanical Engineer, Mr J. Clayton, his personal assistant, Mr A.D. Jones, Locomotive Running Superintendent, Mr F. Bushrod, Chief Assistant Operating Superintendent and Mr F.V. Milton, Assistant Advertising Manager. The load on the

down journey consisted of 12 of the latest eight-wheeled coaches including two dining cars. Tare weight was 392 tons and with a full complement of passengers and luggage, made up to about 430 tons. Schedule times were closely adhered to and no attempt was made to 'extend' the engine:

'Speed reached 60 mph at Surbiton and 67 mph on the very slight descent to Esher, while 68 mph was attained on 1¼ miles of 1 in 330 down past Weybridge. The continuous rise of 10½ miles from Byfleet Junction to mile-post 31, gradually increasing in steepness from 1 in 388 to 1 in 300, reduced the speed to 49 mph and after a sustained rate of 62½ to 60 mph on the undulating stretch that ensues to the 46 mile-post, the 6-mile ascent at 1 in 249 to the junctions at Worting resulted in a minimum of 47½mph. On the 1 in 178 fall to Andover the maximum speed of the journey was attained – 83 mph – and below Porton 77½ mph was reached; on the intervening rise to Grateley, comprising 3 miles at about 1 in 240 and 2¾ at 1 in 165, speed did not fall below 52 mph. The fact that only ½ minute was gained on schedule time with such intermediate speeds as this is a testimony to the arduous character of this schedule of 90 minutes for the journey of 83.8 miles.

'On the return journey the train was due to leave Salisbury at 2.28pm (working time) but, owing to a late arrival from the West of England, the actual start was 8½ minutes behind time. As before, the load consisted of 12 coaches, but in this case included two vehicles of lighter tare, the empty weight behind the tender being 388 tons, and the gross load about 415 tons. The initial booking of 22 min to Andover is extremely hard, and as the policy of working the engine under easy steam was adhered to, there was a loss of 2¾ min on this stage. But the loss was considerably more than recouped by a remarkable exhibition of speed from Andover to Waterloo, whereby the engine gained 9¼ minutes with this heavy train. There is a 10-mile ascent from the Salisbury start: in its early stages at 1 in 733-610, the engine accelerated to 37½mph; up 2½ miles at 1 in 169 and 1¼ at 1 in 140, past Porton, speed was maintained steadily at the same rate; on 1¾ miles at 1 in 245 it rose to 41½ mph; and up the final stretch at 1 in 735-440 50 mph was reached. Maximum rate at Andover was 74mph and a fine ascent was then made of the rising grades beyond, with a fall from 74 to 59 mph up 3¼ miles at 1 in 178, and from 66 to 60 up 1¼ miles at 1 in 194 to Hurstbourne. All the way up the 1 in 550 from there to the summit of the rise, near Worting, speed

E853 SIR RICHARD GRENVILLE at Battersea (where, incidentally, very few views of the Nelsons come to light) with one of the six wheel tenders, of which there are very few views. The picture illustrates well the panel on the rear of the tender employed through the various (green) Southern liveries. The numberplate on the tender rear, like the cabside plate, had a red ground. Photograph H.C. Casserley, courtesy R.M. Casserley.

Malachite green on LORD NELSON at Southampton on 21 October 1950, showing how the number was painted on the tender rear. Photograph H.C. Casserley, courtesy R.M. Casserley.

remained steadily at the 60 mph mark. From there onwards to Surbiton speed ranged between 79 mph below Basingstoke, 71½ at Hook, 77½ at Fleet, 69 at mile-post 31, 80½ – the maximum – between Woking and Byfleet and 71½ from Weybridge to Esher; speed was then dropped to a little over 60mph from Surbiton to the service slack through Clapham Junction. A clear road was obtained into Waterloo, where the train arrived only 2 min late having regained 6½ min on booked time from Salisbury.

Certain of the times on the up journey are worthy of special comment. The time occupied by the engine over the 68.9 miles from Grateley to Clapham Junction was precisely one hour. The 36 miles from Worting Junction to Esher were covered in 29 min 15 sec at an average speed of 73.8 mph. Save for a momentary fall to 69 at mile-post 31, speed did not fall below 70 mph for the whole of the distance just mentioned, and the rate remained in excess of 60 mph for some 67 miles continuously – from below Grateley to the usual Clapham Junction slack – except for a momentary 59 between Andover and Whitchurch. That the engine was far from being worked hard, even on the up journey, is evidenced by the fact that the driver (Francis, of Eastleigh) was working almost the whole way from Grateley to Waterloo on 15 per cent cut-off, with the regulator partly closed except on the ascent from Andover; the bank from Salisbury was negotiated at about 25 per cent cut-off with full regulator. It may be further remarked that the exhaust of the engine, except for a few moments after starting, was inaudible from the leading coach; an occasional escape of steam from the safety-valves also showed that no pressing demands were being made on the boiler. On such results as these it is clear that the working of 500-ton trains at average speeds of 55mph for which the 'Lord Nelson' class has been designed, will prove a matter of no difficulty.'

A new modern locomotive excited interest all over the country and less than a fortnight later LORD NELSON was providing a short footplate trip for the Duke and Duchess of York (the future King George VI and Queen Elizabeth the Queen Mother) on an official visit to Ashford Works. Appropriately enough (the connection would not have been lost on the PR men) 21 October was Trafalgar Day, as Townroe points out.

All this of course came only after some careful evaluation, very much less in the public eye; LORD NELSON had been ordered in June 1925 and seems to have emerged from Eastleigh (in works grey livery) around 12 August 1926, making a trial run to Micheldever the following day. Bradley details all this: on 14th and 15th it worked five coach specials to Brockenhurst where on the second occasion a tender bearing ran hot. Over the next few days the tender gave more trouble than the

engine and on return to works new bogies were fitted. Fully painted, LORD NELSON came back out into the daylight on 21 September 1926. It would be nearly two years before the second Nelson appeared; the delay would have unexpected and doleful effects, as we shall see…

During that time LORD NELSON was put through coal consumption tests, on ordinary service trains which formed a programme of 'ironing out' faults before the 'production' run began. 'No.850 worked all the principal trains on the Eastern and Western Sections' writes Townroe. The 500 tons at 55mph ideal was achievable, and on one notable occasion the locomotive took the King of Egypt to Dover on his way home in the 'heaviest single-engined train [ever] to have been worked out of Victoria'.

****

In March 1927 Maunsell had an order for ten King Arthurs changed to ten Lord Nelsons and these were delivered between June 1928 and April 1929; all were from Eastleigh and were given the Order No.E157 (LORD NELSON had been E124) as follows:

E851	SIR FRANCIS DRAKE
E852	SIR WALTER RALEIGH
E853	SIR RICHARD GRENVILLE
E854	HOWARD OF EFFINGHAM
E855	ROBERT BLAKE
E856	LORD St VINCENT
E857	LORD HOWE
E858	LORD DUNCAN
E859	LORD HOOD
E860	LORD HAWKE

Before this production series was very much under way, five more were added to Order No.E348, substitutions in a similar way to the batch of ten, for engines already ordered. There were to be ten Lord Nelsons and fifteen Schools, but this was adjusted, Bradley describes, to five Nelsons, ten Schools and ten U1 2-6-0s. The last five Nelsons, built from September through to November 1929 were thus (the 'E' went in 1931):

E861	LORD ANSON
E862	LORD COLLINGWOOD
E863	LORD RODNEY
E864	SIR MARTIN FROBISHER
E865	SIR JOHN HAWKINS

****

The Lord Nelsons were an excellent design, a wonder of fitting power within existing weight/loading gauge restrictions on a par with any since as ingenuity and new materials enabled ever more power within a 19th century loading gauge, rather like CORONATION later or BRITANNIA after that. Yet they did not make the impact they should have, though they were capable of excellent individual

performances. The problem, as seen so often throughout locomotive history, was one of numbers. To employ a somewhat inappropriate expression for the period, the class (like any other) needed a 'critical mass' to be effective. And in one way, oddly, Maunsell's careful introduction of the design didn't help. One locomotive, as Winkworth eloquently points out, is not much use to an Operating Department (shades of DUKE OF GLOUCESTER). 'More of an embarrassment' he calls them (single locomotives, that is) for no alterations can be made to any schedules and no crews get used to it while all crews (who only meet with it now and then) are unfamiliar with the thing and remember only the unfamiliar and therefore awkward bits. Moreover, spares are available only intermittently and fitters unfamiliar in any event. LORD NELSON's fate was to be around long enough for everyone to get to dislike it. When the rest of the class came, there were still not sufficient numbers to firmly establish the Nelsons as the new generation of top express power.

They were said to be poor steamers at times and, fatally to any engineman's verdict, not obviously and substantially superior to what they replaced – in this case, the King Arthurs. Perhaps Firemen could not get used to the split level firebox and again, numbers would have solved this, for crews would have got them day in and day out. Moreover, there was a disappointing record of mechanical failure. Much of the work was a long way from the 500 tons at 55mph 'gold standard'. As Winkworth points out, a mere sixteen engines (it had been intended at one time that there would be twenty-six of them but in the event the finances didn't stretch) could not even be made into two links, so while one link was contrived at Stewarts Lane it meant that, so far as the Western Section was concerned, it merely had a few Lord Nelsons 'knocking about'.

It was Bulleid's alterations in the 1930s and 1940s – the tenders, new cylinders with different ports and passages, Lemaître exhausts, new grate and ashpan arrangements – that put the Lord Nelsons on a better footing and the LSW main line saw a good deal of better running. The prospect of greatly improved working was destroyed by the War, however; the works had much else to do and speeds and times were cut back. In February 1940 the Nelsons were concentrated at Nine Elms; two years later a number went to Bournemouth to replace Schools 4-4-0s and the class finished the war divided between the two sheds, 'Bomo' and Nine Elms. They were concentrated in a 'fleet' as they should have been from the first but still the old numbers problem remained. Moreover, come the peace the very best jobs were in the hands of the Merchant Navy Pacifics

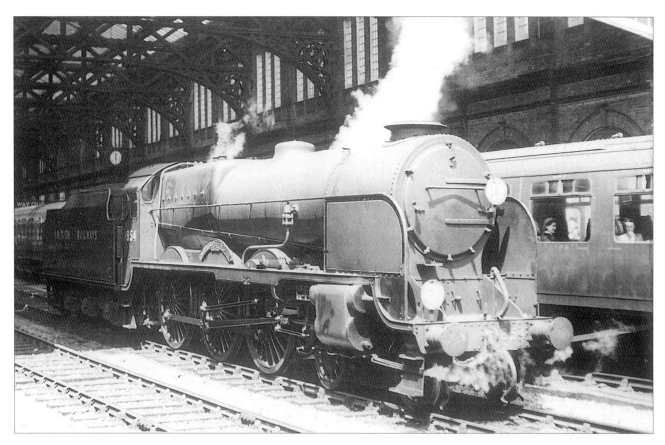

and numbers of light Pacifics were becoming available for every duty. LORD NELSON, once indeed 'the most powerful passenger locomotive in the country' and its compatriots now formed the Second Division of the Bournemouth and Salisbury lines. And this was the story of their BR careers; power classification was upped from 6P to 7P in 1951 when BR created the 8P classification for the biggest engines but much of the work could hardly compare to what many similarly classified 7P locomotives were doing – Royal Scots, A3s, Castles and so on.

****

BR found a similar predicament in 1948 to that experienced by the SR in 1923 – namely different groups of locomotives with a degree of overlap with respect to numbers. So, until a comprehensive renumbering was drawn up and implemented, a letter was added to denote the former owner, 'S' for Southern, 'E' for LNE and so on. The letter was applied as the loco passed through works but by late March 1948 the familiar full renumbering scheme commenced, though WR engines were not affected. By this time no more than about 10% of engines had acquired the letter prefix; on the SR some 125 got an 'S' (actually smaller than the numbers) including our 854. It was the only Nelson so affected – in contrast 21 light Pacifics got it! So from March 1948 and for a couple of years you could see three categories of numbers: engines not yet altered, so still running with old company number; engines with 'S' prefix and engines fully renumbered. Here is the unique s854 HOWARD OF EFFINGHAM in the shadows of Bournemouth Central.

30864 SIR MARTIN FROBISHER in the 1948 experimental apple green (also applied to 30856 and 30861) and officially lined in red/cream/grey. In reality the SR was short of cream so yellow was used instead. Smoke deflectors and wheels were black and tender lining stops short at the curved top. They worked together with plum and spilt milk coach sets between Waterloo and Bournemouth. Photograph R.K. Blencowe Collection.

Above. 861 LORD ANSON getting readied for the road at Eastleigh shed. The agile fitter's mate is clambering under the boiler to reach the inside gear. This emphasises the absurdity of the 135 degree crank setting of a Nelson which necessitated four sets of valve gear with two of them unavoidably tucked away inside. The advantages of this were small beer compared to the extra maintenance burden of largely hidden machinery. The 90 degree setting and two (only) sets of gear, with rocking shafts to the inside piston valves, would have been more logical. It was employed extensively elsewhere after all, such as on the Princess Coronations and, for that matter, on the Paddleboxes. Photograph H.N. Shepherd, The Transport Treasury.

The BR version. 30853 SIR RICHARD GRENVILLE with AWS and speedometer, at Waterloo in September 1961. Note loss of snifting valves from the smokebox and the first BR emblem; the odd thing is that when 30853 got its new front end in 1958, its tender had the second emblem. A tender change about a year later saw the return of the original, as here! This it took to the grave, in 1962. Photograph Jack Kirke, The Transport Treasury.

A familiar (but none the worse for that) Brian Morrison view. 30857 LORD HOWE, long past its taper boiler days and with ten inch numbers, shunts vans at Clapham Junction on 25 April 1954. Power class 'A' now on cabside, a BR change. Photograph Brian Morrison.

Looking beautiful, 30854 HOWARD OF EFFINGHAM at its by-then home shed, Eastleigh on 25 August 1957. BR dark green and second tender emblem; 'flat' front under the smokebox. A good view of how the cylinder drain pipes (dribbling!) were set into a casing on the front steps. Shows the 'economy' straight lining on the valence of the running plate. Photograph R.C. Riley, The Transport Treasury.

30858 LORD DUNCAN at Nine Elms, 17 August 1956. Note how, with the new Bulleid cylinders, the steam pipes no longer project through the smoke deflectors. Soon into the BR regime the Nelsons were made power class 6P, shortly raised to 7P. LORD DUNCAN has the old 'A' below the ten inch number and the new '7P' above it. Photograph J. Robertson, The Transport Treasury.

30858 LORD DUNCAN on a Waterloo-Bournemouth train at Medstead & Four Marks on 8 May 1955, on what is now the Mid-Hants preserved line. The train had been diverted from the main line, probably for engineering purposes; despite the line being single it was nevertheless quite suited, with its passing loops, to bigger engines and longer trains. Photograph R.C. Riley, The Transport Treasury.

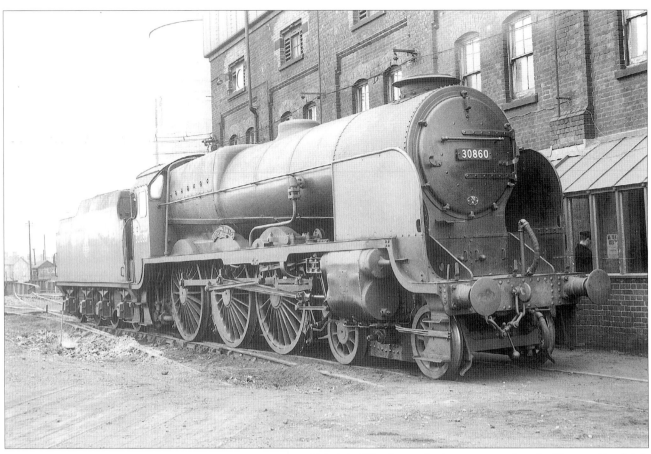

Looking gigantic as no other British 4-6-0 could, 30860 LORD HAWKE alongside the water tank and offices at Eastleigh shed (turntable in background) on 28 April 1958. The class was occupied throughout the 1950s on not too onerous duties on the Western Section, mainly the London-Weymouth route. Winkworth has looked in detail at their running in the spring of 1954, and has worked out that half the class was not in use in a typical week while the other half amassed over 13,000 miles a week – an average of 813 miles per engine. It lost the long barrel boiler in March 1955, never to regain it, so appears here with a standard one. Photograph Frank Hornby.

It was in the last months of the Southern Railway that the Lord Nelsons extended their sphere of operation, to begin working to Oxford and back with Bournemouth trains, via Reading West. On 27 February 1954 30861 LORD ANSON has turned at Oxford ex-GW shed (out of sight to the left) and is running back through the station right way round for its train back south. The WR engine is 6937 CONYNGHAM HALL. Photograph R.C. Riley, The Transport Treasury.

DETAILS, DIFFERENCES AND CHANGES

There were of course a sequence of modifications to the Lord Nelsons, almost from the first; they continued through Bulleid's reign after Maunsell's retirement. Under both engineers it was a process of improvement and/or experimentation. I've tried to sum them up in the usual 'Book Of' manner…

LORD HOOD's Wheels

No.E859 LORD HOOD appeared with 6ft 3in driving wheels, instead of the 6ft 7in of the rest of the Lord Nelsons. Townroe ascribes this to the idea, one that Maunsell was obviously well acquainted with, that smaller diameter driving wheels should be of greater efficacy on heavily graded routes, like the LSW west of Salisbury, and cites the example of Drummond 4-4-0s with 6ft instead of 6ft 7in driving wheels, intended for just such work. In Winkworth's highly detailed account – probably the best there is, by a fair way – it is revealed that the original proposal had been 6ft 0in, for use on the *Eastern* Section. Whatever the origins, apparently this would have meant too much work compensating elsewhere for the dimensional changes, so 6ft 3in was settled on. This reduction of four inches produced no difference in

working, despite an indicated increase in tractive effort, either on the Eastern or Western Sections, where LORD HOOD was tried against other Nelsons.

LORD HAWKE's Boiler

Maunsell had seemingly-significant changes made to both the last two of the batch of ten. LORD HOOD (above) had the smaller wheels and E860 LORD HAWKE had a longer boiler. Tubes were longer by ten inches than the stock 13ft 9in tubes at Eastleigh but no increased performance was to be found. As Townroe puts it, the answer (to increased tube length) was… 'a lemon'. The Nelsons, before Bulleid made further smokebox alterations which got rid of them, had a noticeable 'piano front' between the frames, covering the inside cylinders. E860 had a flat front, prefiguring later developments for the class a whole. Boiler no.860 made a limited way round the class in later years.

SIR WALTER RALEIGH's Window Wiper – Driver's Side

This Bulleidesque device appeared on 852 SIR WALTER RALEIGH when it got its new high tender in November 1937. It functioned like a latter day road vehicle wiper/washer except that it took

hot water off the injector. It presumably disappeared in the War. Apparently they all got it, though it is certainly difficult to see in photographs.

Bogie

A deeper frame bogie appears around the mid-1930s, illustrated a couple of times in 'Excellent to a Degree' earlier on.

Washout Plugs

There were eight plugs on the left-hand firebox side (looking forward) and seven on the other side. The two rows were staggered relative to each other in accordance with normal practice.

Smoke Deflectors

These were first fitted on E850 in the middle of 1929; the fitting does not show on the Record Cards, such as they are, but the rest seem to have been dealt with on the next works visit. The second batch, of five, had them from new.

Lamp Irons

Before smoke deflectors appeared, the two intermediate lamp irons projected out from the smokebox rim at mid-height; once the deflectors were fitted, the irons were moved up slightly but the discs projected out and obscured

Splendid portrait of 30852 at Bournemouth shed, in BR green with the long boiler, no.860 originally fitted to E860 LORD HAWKE. In this livery the cylinders were black, with vertical orange lines front and rear. SIR WALTER carries a Merchant Navy chimney. Photograph W.G. Boyden, courtesy Frank Hornby.

E Numbers
The 'E' prefix denoted an engine allocated to Eastleigh for repairs. This was dropped in 1931. D.W. Winkworth, a true delver compared to my poor efforts, has probably examined as many photographs of Southern locos as anyone, and reveals that the 'E', though it did not appear at first on the bufferbeam, it did so for a period shortly before its abolition, at least on some engines. Before the 'E' 'N°' had sufficed on one side of the drawhook, the number on the other – see Liveries.

SIR JOHN's cranks
The Lord Nelsons had 135° crank settings, as remarked earlier, that gave a unique eight separate exhaust beats per revolution of the coupled wheels – see the handy *Railway Gazette* diagram in the Appendix. It was a background of difficulty, perhaps, that prompted Maunsell to try a number of modifications and one of them was to adopt the traditional 90°, on 865 SIR JOHN HAWKINS in late 1933. It was identifiable from the rest from the conventional four exhaust beats per revolution. It also involved a different set of wheel balances, much more prominent than on the others. No merit was found in the alteration and ever after it bore a reputation for heavier than usual coal consumption, though pre-War Top Link Nine Elms Driver Payne considered it a favourite.

LORD COLLINGWOOD's Chimney
862 LORD COLLINGWOOD emerged from Eastleigh in August 1934 with a double chimney and modified Kylchap twin exhausts of the in-line type. While this sort of arrangement found huge success elsewhere something was 'missing' in this particular application and no obvious improvement was found. At this juncture it might be worth noting what Dr W.A. Tuplin had to say in *Railway World* in April 1959: *It is hard to believe that anyone really thought that these changes could possibly make any perceptible difference to performance and they certainly did not. It is significant that the one thing that was obviously at fault [he meant the firebox] was not altered, even in the special boilers, and so one is inclined to believe that Maunsell was trying not to put the Nelsons right bur rather to prove how good the original design was by showing that no change that anyone suggested could effect any improvement.*

SIR JOHN HAWKINS' Chimney
No.865 SIR JOHN HAWKINS was fitted with a double blastpipe in March 1938. The arrangement on 862 LORD COLLINGWOOD was amended and both were tested on the Bournemouth line. Both performed better than the other engines in the class but not dramatically so, it would seem.

Lemaître Exhaust
In order to pursue further tests, 863 LORD RODNEY got a wide stovepipe chimney (without multiple jet exhaust) in June 1938. Various alterations proved fruitless until multiple jet exhausts were fitted. 'By mid-1938 863 was equipped with what in due course evolved into the standard fitment known as the Lemaître exhaust' writes Winkworth in *Maunsell's Nelsons*. 'Contrary to popular belief, the large diameter chimney was introduced before the multiple jet arrangement.' Others were enrolled into the experiments, 855, 856, 861 and 864 getting the 23in stovepipe chimneys. After a year a standard fitting was arrived at and during 1939 all had been equipped with the Lemaître exhaust:

850	6/39
851	6/39
852	4/39
853	4/39
854	6/39
855	9/39
856	8/39
857	10/39
858	5/39
859	5/39
860	12/39
861	10/39
862	5/39
863	6/39
864	6/39
865	6/39

New Cylinders for Old
As well as the new exhausts for the Nelsons, Bulleid rearranged the grates and ashpans too for better airflow; next came the cylinders and the engines were in effect subtly rebuilt. 851 SIR FRANCIS DRAKE received new cylinders in June 1939 with revised layout with revised ports and passages. Bulleid had ordered 10in piston valves but this first conversion, 851 got 8in ones instead, keeping them to the end. The rest got the 10in version or rather, were to get them. The War came and work was delayed, while 863 never got the new cylinders at all – 853 got them as late as 1958. With the exception of 851 with its 'non-standard' new cylinders and 863 which never got them, the new cylinders brought about one or two distinctive visual variations. On all except 851 and 853 the smokebox was extended slightly so that the 'piano' front over the cylinders disappeared – something that had only been seen so far on 857 and 860, the two with non-standard boilers. On the engines

equipped with the new standard cylinders the steam pipes no longer projected through the smoke deflectors but were out of sight behind them:

850: new cylinders 3/42, loses piano front
851: new cylinders 6/39 but non-standard, retains piano front
852: new cylinders 3/40, loses piano front
853: new cylinders 2/58, loses piano front
854: new cylinders 11/46, loses piano front
855: new cylinders 12/40, loses piano front
856: new cylinders 7/40, loses piano front
857: new cylinders 10/39, piano front already gone
858: new cylinders 1/51, loses piano front
859: new cylinders 12/46, loses piano front
860: new cylinders 12/39, piano front already gone
861: new cylinders 8/43, loses piano front
862: new cylinders 4/40, loses piano front
863: no new cylinders, retains piano front to the end
864: new cylinders 5/48, loses piano front
865: new cylinders 9/40, loses piano front

LORD HOWE's Boiler
In 1937 857 LORD HOWE appeared with a unique taper boiler, no.1063, looking as it strained the very limits of the loading gauge. It had a round top firebox wholly unlike the rest of the class. A combustion chamber extended into the boiler barrel provided, it was said, to gain experience for an upcoming Pacific design, 'although at the time' Winkworth writes, 'some play was made of it being an improvement on the Lord Nelson class'. The boiler was quite unmistakable and though it looked bigger, in actual fact the boiler between tubeplates was actually shorter, by a foot. There was one snifting valve, behind the chimney, in contrast to the two, one either side of the smokebox, on the rest of the Nelsons. For the first period that no.1063 was carried (January 1937-September 1941) smoke deflectors were 'cranked'; for the second period (January 1943-February 1945) they remained standard.

Snifting Valves
The 'snifting valves' were prominent either side of the chimney, except in the case of the taper boiler no.1063 on 857 LORD HOWE, which had one only, behind the chimney. From 1947 they were deemed not to warrant the maintenance time and money involved and they were dispensed with, beginning with 861 and 863; the last to lose them was 857 in 1949.

Speed Recorders and Speedometer
All the Nelsons had Flaman speed recorders; the equipment took its readings from the right-hand rear coupled wheel and provided a continuous record on a paper roll as well as an indication for the Driver. The first one appeared on 855 when it got its tall sided tender in August 1938; the class was equipped with the recorders as follows:

vision
vision that was already somewhat restricted so they were moved again 'inboard', to the smokebox door itself. At the same time, it would seem, a small handle on the right-hand side of the door (looking from the cab) was removed to make way for the right-hand iron. Afterwards you opened the door by grasping the lamp iron.

30862 LORD COLLINGWOOD on a shortish train at Eastleigh, 15 August 1956. Whatever the ranking of the Nelsons and their duties, Eastleigh shed always seemed to keep them clean and presentable and generally they did not acquire the unkempt look until the very last year or so. Some observers have found the big Bulleid chimneys 'clumsy' but probably most of us feel that they sat well with the Maunsell and Bulleid types. Photograph J. Robertson, The Transport Treasury.

850	9/38	30858	-	30863	10/59
851	6/39	30859	-	30864	10/59
852	4/39	30860	12/60	30865	-
853	4/39	30861	12/59		
854	2/39	30862	5/61		
855	8/38	30863	-		
856	11/38	30864	-		
857	10/38	30865	-		
858	5/39				
859	11/38				
860	12/39				
861	11/38				
862	10/38				
863	11/38				
864	11/38				
865	6/39				

The recorders were removed, deemed an unnecessary luxury in wartime and they were not refitted. Years passed until a programme of fitting speedometers, applied across many BR classes, was begun in 1959. This time it was the familiar equipment attached to the left-hand rear driving wheel. It was late in the day of course and not all the Nelsons got it; dates are as follows:

30850	12/60
30851	9/60
30852	8/60
30853	4/60
30854	-
30855	6/60
30856	9/60
30857	7/60

AWS

Automatic Warning System again came late in the day and again not all the locomotives lasted long enough to get it. The battery box was variously on the left-hand side on the running plate. Some got the AWS but not the speedometer (though where fitted, it was always at the same time as the AWS) while one, 30865, got neither. An unusual external manifestation of the AWS on the Nelsons was a pair of holes low down on the left-hand cab sheet. Fitting was as follows:

30850	12/60
30851	9/60
30852	8/60
30853	4/60
30854	10/59
30855	6/60
30856	9/60
30857	7/60
30858	10/59
30859	9/59
30860	12/60
30861	12/59
30862	5/61

Livery

LORD NELSON itself, of course, started life in works grey but very quickly acquired the standard SR 'Maunsell' green, otherwise called 'sage green'. Lining was black and white with yellow lettering. The work was intricate, with duly lined out green cylinders (bands front and aft) and steps and even the green 'splashers' over the bogie wheels. The Nelsons had cab numberplates; like the name plates, the background was painted red. Tenders had SOUTHERN with the engine number painted below. In 1938 855 and 862 appeared with panels on the cylinders instead of conventional lining. As mentioned elsewhere, the front number was painted on the bufferbeam, prefaced by 'N°' on the other side of the drawhook. The 'N°' was dropped when the 'E' prefix appeared and then reappeared when the 'E' in turn was dropped in 1931. In this new incarnation, the 'N°' had the underline set higher, with a dot underneath it. The later smoke deflectors were black, like the smokebox.

In 1938 olive green appears, with cylinders plain black, on some engines. Lining was yellow and dark green with

No	850	851	852	853	854	855	856	857	858	859	860	861	862	863	864	865
Olive Green	-	-	4/39	-	2/39	11/38	11/38	-	5/39	5/39	-	11/38	-	11/38	-	-
Malachite Green	6/39	6/39	-	4/39	6/39	9/39	8/39	10/39	5/40	1/40	12/39	10/39	5/39	6/39	6/39	6/39
Black	4/44	1/44	6/42	2/43	12/43	4/43	9/42	1/43	9/42	9/42	10/42	8/43	11/42	6/43	6/43	5/43
Malachite Green	11/46	11/46	3/47	6/47	11/46	5/47	6/46A	6/46	3/46	12/46	1/47	11/47A	8/48	9/46	2/47A	6/46
BR No.	11/48	1/49	3/49	11/48	6/49B	2/49	4/48	12/49	6/48	2/49	11/48	5/48	8/48	8/49	5/48	8/48
BR Green	1/51	10/50	12/51	7/50	10/51	9/50	4/50	12/49	1/51	3/51	10/50	3/50	2/51	8/49	4/51	11/49

A – Apple Green: 30856 in 6/48, 30861 and 30864 in 5/48

B – 'S' prefix 3/48

cylinders and smoke deflectors black. The number plates were replaced by numbers painted on the cab side; 'N°' was finally dropped.

Nelson livery afterwards becomes a minor Vale of Tears for anyone demanding absolute historical precision, as malachite green appears and then wartime black. Some Nelsons went from olive to malachite to black, others didn't get the malachite and went straight to black while others went sage to malachite to black without ever getting the olive. When you add in lining variations, as Bradley puts it, there were 'so many variations of the theme that the only features common to all were the large gilt buffer beam numerals, SOUTHERN on the tenders and cab numerals'.

Reversion to malachite green began in March 1946 and was complete in 1948. So far as post-War reversion to malachite green is concerned, all the Nelsons were dealt with in 1946 or 1947, except 862 which was still black when nationalised. From January 1948 until August 1949 repaints were in malachite with BR markings and the majority during this time received full malachite, the second application post-War. Until late 1948 tenders were lettered BRITISH RAILWAYS after which they were left blank. Where only a part paint was undertaken, SOUTHERN remained as on 30858 (see LORD DUNCAN subsequently illustrated). No Lord Nelson got the BR emblem until it received the dark green.

Three, 30856, 30861 and 30864 bore a trial BR apple green livery along with the spirits of the time in 1948. The Nelsons avoided the blue and got the BR dark (in reality GW) green from the summer of 1949.

The table (above) is made up from a more comprehensive one first set out by D.W. Winkworth in *Maunsell's Nelsons* and subsequently amended in the light of later discoveries (personally communicated by Mr D.W. Winkworth and Mr E.S. Youldon, for which many thanks).

A Note on Boilers

Eleven boilers were built for the eleven locos 850-860 and given the same numbers as the engines on which they were first used. Five boilers were next built for the five locos 861-865 and given numbers 817-821.

Another boiler was built in December 1930 as a spare and numbered 822. It was first used on 850 LORD NELSON.

A further boiler was built in December 1936, the special round firebox top no.1063 for use exclusively on 857 LORD HOWE for two short periods only, 1937-1941 and again 1943-1945. It was scrapped at Brighton W/E 26/1/52.

A last Nelson boiler 'proper' had been built in June 1934 as a further spare; it was first used on 863 LORD RODNEY.

(Note: boiler no.860 was the long barrel one first used on 860 LORD HAWKE and confined to that loco until August 1955 when it saw service on 30855 until 1958 and then on 30852 until withdrawn.)

TENDERS: 'A Mixed Bag'

Perhaps the most confusing area of

Malachite green for the old sea dog at Nine Elms on 26 July 1947. When this livery disappeared, the Lord Nelsons never looked as bright and cheerful again. Once the engines were concentrated on the Western Section with a relatively tight sphere of operation the old familiarity problems in firing the long box would have eased; this, together with the Bulleid changes, would improve performance though of course the duties, for a 7P locomotive, remained relatively light. 'It is not without significance', R.C. Riley writes, 'that when the late Driver Bert Hooker retired his colleagues asked what he wanted as a presentation and he chose a model Lord Nelson'. It should be said that during the early post-War years the Nelsons, until early 1949, were major players from Bournemouth shed where ten were based. Their association with Eastleigh shed didn't start until 1949 when Bournemouth got its first Pacifics, new Merchant Navys 35025-35030. Photograph The Transport Treasury.

Table to show movement of boilers, constructed from surviving records of boiler attention. It gives a good indication of works visits and General Overhauls. To be read in conjuction with the individual tables given under each locomotive. Compiled by E.S. Youldon.

Loco	First Boiler	Subsequent Boilers
850	850 8/26	822 (new) 12/30; 851 10/32; 819 5/35; 856 4/37; 855 6/39; 819 4/44; 850 1/46; 1234 11/46; 853 11/48; 856 1/51; 857 2/54; 851 3/57; 821 1/59
851	851 6/28	853 4/31; 859 2/33; 855 12/34; 822 10/36; 858 1/42; 852 12/43; 857 3/45; 821 3/46; 856 2/49; 1234 10/50; 854 10/52; 821 12/55; 820 12/59
852	852 7/28	817 10/35; 819 11/37; 851 2/40; 818 7/44; 859 9/45; 818 3/47; 821 3/49; 820 2/50; 859 10/53; 860 10/58
853	853 9/28	850 3/31; 857 5/34; 851 2/36; 859 4/39; 817 9/40; 1234 2/43; 854 10/44; 858 1/46; 819 5/47; 1234 11/48; 850 6/50; 819 1/55; 857 3/58
854	854 10/28	822 11/32; 853 6/36; 818 2/39; 852 5/41; 857 11/43; 853 3/45; 1234 6/45; 822 11/46; 819 6/49; 818 8/54; 817 5/57
855	855 11/28	854 6/33; 818 9/37; 1234 8/38; 859 12/40; 820 4/43; 856 3/44; 858 6/47; 821 9/50; 860 7/55; 819 9/58
856	856 11/28	855 3/32; 856 7/32; 853 4/33; 857 3/36; 821 6/38; 854 7/40; 822 9/42; 855 7/46; 822 2/52; 853 9/58; 856 8/60
857	857 12/28	820 9/33; 1063 (new) 1/37; 820 9/41; 1063 1/43; 852 3/45; 857 6/46; 859 8/47; 852 7/52; 817 9/55; 822 9/58
858	858 1/29	859 5/31; 854 12/32; 856 4/33; 852 3/36; 817 3/38; 819 5/40; 854 9/42; 855 7/44; 819 4/46; 817 5/47; 854 1/51; 851 3/52; 1234 12/56; 1234 3/59
859	859 3/29	853 4/31; 855 7/32; 850 7/34; 855 11/36; 850 11/38; 856 1/40; 818 4/42; 858 4/44; 818 11/45; 851 12/46; 857 2/48; 822 6/49; 817 3/51; 850 5/55; 859 9/59
860	860 4/29	850 12/36; 860 8/37; 855 3/55; 853 12/60
861	817 9/29	859 7/35; 857 11/38; 821 8/43; 854 2/46; 856 11/47; 820 1/49; 852 2/50; 855 6/52; 856 3/56; 851 11/59
862	818 10/29	858 8/33; 853 7/37; 854 1/38; 853 4/40; 850 7/43; 853 11/45; 854 12/48; 858 12/50; 820 3/54; 858 5/54; 820 12/55; 858 4/61
863	819 10/29	818 10/33; 1234 (new) 6/34; 858 6/38; 1234 12/40; 819 11/42; 853 2/44; 851 2/45; 852 9/46; 818 8/49; 858 5/54; 818 9/57; 822 3/61; 822 3/61
864	820 11/29	821 1/34; 818 2/35; 820 4/37; 821 4/41; 817 6/43; 850 1/47; 851 5/48; 853 4/51; 854 7/56; 854 11/57
865	821 11/29	819 12/33; 821 3/35; 852 3/38; 850 9/40; 859 5/43; 820 3/45; 850 8/48; 857 10/49; 1234 3/53; 852 7/57

All dates are ex-works dates.

Loco	withdrawn	Final boiler and its fate
30850	8/62	821 preserved with loco
30851	12/61	820 cut up Eastleigh 5/5/62
30852	2/62	860 cut up Ashford 17/2/62
30853	3/62	857 cut up Eastleigh 23/6/62
30854	9/61	817 sold 2/12/61
30855	9/61	819 sold 12/5/62
30856	9/62	856 cut up Eastleigh 15/12/62
30857	9/62	850 cut up Eastleigh 24/11/62
30858	8/61	1234 sold 12/5/62
30859	12/61	859 sold 5/5/62
30860	8/62	853 cut up Eastleigh 13/10/62
30861	10/62	851 cut up Eastleigh 15/12/62
30862	10/62	858 cut up Eastleigh 15/12/62
30863	2/62	822 cut up Ashford c2/62
30864	1/62	854 cut up Eastleigh 23/6/62
30865	5/61	852 sold 2/12/61

Boilers condemned ahead of loco
818 last used on 30863; sold 23/9/61
855 last used on 30860; sold 30/9/61
1063 last used on 857; cut up Brighton 26/1/52

detail variation in the Nelsons concerns the tenders. The first, on LORD NELSON (the one that had its bogies and drawgear altered after trials) was, in Winkworth's words 'a cleaned up version of the bogie type attached to the King Arthur class'. It was flat sided, with a capacity of five tons and 5,000 gallons, with prominent vacuum reservoirs at the rear.

The first 'batch', the ten engines E851-E860, got a mixture of tenders. They had, after all, been substituted for ten King Arthurs; these were to have had six wheel 4,000 gallon tenders for use on the Eastern Section and the order proceeded because the Nelsons too, it was thought, would work in the east. However, five, E851, E854, E855, E856 and E857 went instead to Nine Elms for Western Section duties and so had to have larger tenders. These were second-hand flat sided 5,000 gallon tenders off S15 4-6-0s 833-837.

Of the other five, however, not all got the six wheel 4,000 gallon tenders; only E852 and E853 got these while the other three, E858, E859 and E860, found themselves with Urie 5,000 gallon tenders with curved top edges.

The second batch, of five, E861-E865, had flat sided 5,000 gallon tenders after the fashion of the original E850. So certainly Winkworth's description, 'mixed bag' is an apt one. But this was not all. The smaller 4,000 gallon tenders were of inadequate capacity and the

two on E852 and E853 were replaced by 5,000 gallon tenders with curved top edges in December 1929 and February 1930 respectively. This meant five, E852 and E853, along with E858, E859 and E860, had the tenders with curved tops; these in turn soon got flat sided tenders instead, ex-King Arthurs 768-772

E852 7/31
E853 3/32
E858 7/32
E859 7/32
E860 6/31

This information comes from Bradley's RCTS *Locos of the SR Vol. One*. Bradley and Eric Youldon eventually sorted out the frenzied tender swops of 1928-1932 involving Nelsons, Schools, S15s and N15s. The pair worked at it for weeks but got there in the end so that the bewildering tender merry-go-round of the Lord Nelsons at the time, where they came from and where they went, could be presented in staggering detail. Put briefly, by the summer of 1932 all the Nelsons had 5,000 gallon flat sided tenders. They were numbered 1000-1015 for the run of the class.

The Lord Nelson tenders rode very well – so well in fact, that the usual vibration which brought the coal forward for the Fireman during a journey was largely absent. This meant clambering into the tender to bring it forward. Bulleid, on taking over, thus had the tenders heightened, beginning with 852 SIR WALTER RALEIGH in November 1937. This generally appears in the Record Cards as simply 'self trimming bunker'. The coal space slope had been altered so that the coal would move forward during running and the new tall sides maintained the capacity thus lost. The Nelsons were all so altered, as follows:

850	6/39
851	6/39
852	11/37
853	10/40
854	2/39
855	8/38
856	7/40
857	10/39
858	5/40
859	1/40
860	12/39
861	11/38
862	4/40
863	12/40
864	11/38
865	9/40

LORD NELSON more or less as built, on a boat train about 1928. The view shows well the prominent lamp irons on the smokebox rim; when the deflectors first appeared the irons were moved up (see LORD HOOD on page 61 for instance) but the discs interfered with the driver's lookout and were soon moved 'inboard'. Admiral Lord Nelson was a national hero on a scale difficult to imagine today, especially as communication then was so much less immediate than now. Trafalgar Day, October 21st, passes barely noticed now and the celebrations this bi-centenary year (2005) will be but a faint echo of those in 1905 which took place not only in Britain and the Empire, but in New York, Tokyo and elsewhere. There scarcely could have been a more appropriate or stirring name for the country's most powerful passenger locomotive.

THE RECORD

In the case of the Lord Nelsons, as pointed out already, the record of works visits is fragmentary and it is only possible to present what is available. Readers will immediately note that the Southern Railway record cupboard is particularly bare.

Int Intermediate
LI Light Intermediate
HI Heavy Intermediate
LC Light Casual
HC Heavy Casual
NC Non Classified

Some were upgraded as the work unfolded, which explains such entries as **LI-GO**. Very rarely it was downgraded, e.g. **LC-NC**.

Above. Nine Elms, 8 September 1956. No need for LORD NELSON CLASS on this one! Photograph Brian Morrison.

Below. The engine at Nine Elms, fitted up with indicator shelter for its test runs. Photograph H.C. Casserley, courtesy R.M. Casserley.

30850 LORD NELSON

To traffic 8/1926

26/2/29-18/5/29**G**	Motion, piston rings, inside cylinders and trailing coupled boxes attended to; 78,073.
12/1930	New 'spare boiler' fitted [boiler no.822 actually built 6/1930]
P/E 22/9/38	Flaman speed recorder
P/E 19/5/39	Large diameter chimney; tender modified
P/E 22/1/42	Bulleid pattern cylinders with 10 inch piston valves
P/E 17/10/48	Renumbered 30850; snifting valves removed
25/1/54-27/2/54**G**	Exhaust injector cone renewed; 117,061
W/E 27/2/54	Tender 1015
11/5/55-3/6/55**LI**	50,115
19-27/10/56**NC-LC**	98,701
22/2/57-23/3/57**G**	111,608
22/12/58-24/1/59**G**	Regulator handle modified, 75,266
1/12/60-31/12/60**LI**	AWS, regulator stuffing box gland and packing, speedometer; 63,870

Sheds
Stewarts Lane from new
Exmouth Junction
(for ACE working) 3-4/30,
then back to Stewarts Lane
Nine Elms 27/2/40
Bournemouth 24/2/43
Eastleigh 8/1/49

Withdrawn 18/8/62; final mileage 1,349,617. Currently being overhauled at Eastleigh Works.

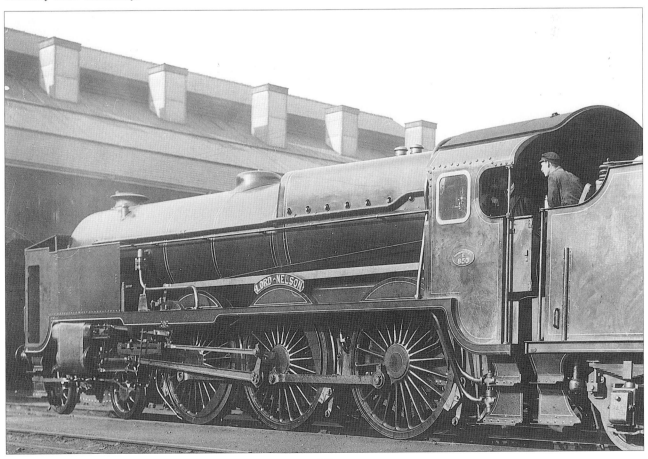

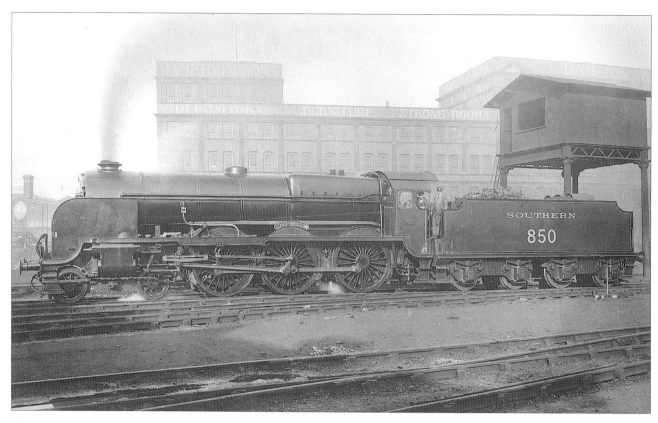

Side on at Stewarts Lane in the mid-1930s. That big boiler was based on that of the Maunsell N mogul, enlarged up to the loading gauge limits. Something that helped the visual impact of the Nelsons was that only a minimal amount of firebox penetrated rearward into the cab. The grate area was the largest of any 4-6-0 in the country, the GWR Kings excepted. Photograph R.S. Carpenter Photos.

LORD NELSON in malachite green at Eastleigh about 1949. That great belpaire firebox, such a distinctive feature of the engines, was only 1ft 6in longer than a King Arthur but the Nelsons (as Townroe points out) required a much greater degree of firing skill, mainly because of the split grate. This was odd, as mentioned already for, while a split grate was unusual for a Southern 4-6-0 and therefore a challenge for a Nelson fireman, it was common elsewhere. All Churchward 4-6-0s apart from the Manors, had them, for instance. The boiler steamed well only if the Fireman had mastered the technique – hence the number of dull runs on record. One of the reasons the Nelsons were kept to so few sheds was the need to get men better acquainted with them.

At times the Nelsons could seem to expand as the eye moved along that boiler... The fire is being thrown out of 30850 LORD NELSON outside the Foreman's office at Eastleigh on 19 August 1950. 'I had hoped' says Jim Aston, 'to get a flying shovel full of red hot clinker in the picture, but the Fireman stopped at the crucial moment'. With BRITISH RAILWAYS on the tender and deflectors now black (compare with the previous picture) the engine is still in SR malachite green, with the tender lining following that top sweep of the tender side. When BR repainted them dark green, the lining, instead of following the edges, was usually taken across horizontally just below where that sheet angled inwards. Some early dark green repaints, however, followed the malachite practice, just to make things awkward. Photograph J.H. Aston.

LORD NELSON on the up 'Cunarder' passing through Winchester in the 1950s. The Cunarder was mostly a Pullman, run in connection with *Queen Mary* and *Queen Elizabeth* sailings. The Nelsons were often utilised on such trains, for it avoided the unfortunate conjunctions possible with the Merchant Navy Pacifics. They were largely kept off these Southampton boat trains – who could imagine ELDERS FYFFES (D.W. Winkworth, *Southern Titled Trains*, D&C, 1988) with its banana boat connotations, heading The Cunarder?.

Two pictures of 30850 LORD NELSON at Nine Elms, with light Pacifics in the background. Both are in near-final condition, in BR green though LORD NELSON has the first tender emblem on 8 September 1956 and the second on 14 March 1959. AWS and speedometer were yet to come. Peter Groom's portrait is unusual in showing the gaps under the boiler. Photographs Brian Morrison, Peter Groom.

30851 SIR FRANCIS DRAKE

To traffic 5/1928

P/E 22/3/39	Self trimming bunker, large diameter chimney, Bullied pattern cylinders 8 inch piston valves, Flaman speed recorder, tender modified
15/2/47-3/4/47**G**	Following the Byfleet derailment of 27/12/46; new motion, bogie, coupled axles, firebox and tender tank
P/E 16/1/49	Renumbered 30851; second set of Bulleid cylinders with 8 inch piston valves, snifting valves removed
1/9/52-18/10/52**G**	
30/12/53-8/1/54**LC**	47,013; boiler barrel plates
8/4/54-15/5/54**G-HI**	54,054
10/11/55-10/12/55**G**	122,248
23/5/57-15/6/57**HI**	
9/7/58-6/9/58**G**	100,588; Regulator handle modified
16/12/59-19/12/59**NC**	44,284
30/8/60-17/9/60**LI**	61,327; AWS, regulator stuffing box and gland, speedometer
29/6/61-30/6/61**NC**	82,160
18/10/60-26/10/61**LC**	

Sheds
Nine Elms from new
Stewarts Lane 6/32
Nine Elms 27/2/40
Bournemouth 24/2/43
Eastleigh 8/1/49

Withdrawn 23/12/61; final mileage 1,296,946. Stored at Eastleigh Works 10/61-4/62, cut up there W/E 5/5/62

851 SIR FRANCIS DRAKE at Southampton Central. The engine had gone new to Nine Elms in 1928 and had moved to Stewarts Lane by mid-1932, so this is presumably the period of the photograph. Sir Francis Drake could hardly be a less well known and celebrated a figure than Nelson, though he was of a different age. Famous for insouciance in finishing his game of bowls as the Armada approached, he was the first man since Magellan to circumnavigate the globe, renaming San Francisco, in the process, Drake's Bay. A great national hero and vanquisher of the Armada. Photograph H.N. Shepherd, The Transport Treasury.

Above. Some close up Nelson detail, courtesy SIR FRANCIS. The smaller version of the front splasher was actually a hinged cover to allow inspection and lubrication of the junction of pivot, radius rod and expansion link beneath. The crosshead and slidebar design was later adopted by Bulleid for his Pacifics. Photograph W. Hermiston, The Transport Treasury.

Below. Inside the shed at Eastleigh, 14 May 1949. SIR FRANCIS is in malachite green with the lined panel on the smoke deflector; it has been renumbered but the tender remains bare. It retains the early bogie – the only Nelson to do so. Photograph J.H. Aston.

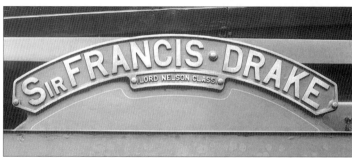

Above. At Nine Elms, 21 May 1957. Photograph J. Robertson, The Transport Treasury.

Out on the road with one of the specials Eastleigh was happy to put in the hands of one of its Nelsons. This is Southampton Central with the down 'Mother Goose' organised by local firm Briggs Motor Bodies Ltd. Photograph D.W. Winkworth.

In the shed yard at Eastleigh (possibly about to use, or having just used, the triangle) on 6 June 1951. Ten inch Gill Sans number – it became eight inch in May 1954. Photograph J.H. Aston.

At Eastleigh shed, 15 August 1956. 30851 had got new cylinders in 1939 but by 'a misunderstanding' got 8 inch instead of 10 inch piston valves. In this way it retained the piano front to the end – like 30863, which never got the new cylinders. This was the one, we remind ourselves, that despite the piano front and original short smokebox there are no steam pipes visible through the smoke deflectors, as should be the case on an 'original'. Photograph J. Robertson, The Transport Treasury.

30852 SIR WALTER RALEIGH
To traffic 7/1928

P/E 16/10/37	Tender altered to self trimming coal bunker
P/E 21/4/39	Large diameter chimney, Flaman speed recorder.
2-3/40	Bulleid pattern cylinders with 10 inch piston valves
18/4/41	Bomb damaged at Nine Elms shed on 18/4/41; frames cut off between the driving and back coupled wheels to facilitate transport from Nine Elms to Eastleigh, new section of framing welded to that which remained. Re-entered service on 18/6/42.
3/1947	Fitted with Neil's rocker bar grates; malachite green
10/1/49-12/3/49**G**	Snifting valves removed, renumbered 30852
28/1/50-28/2/50**HC**	
24/11/51-3/1/52**HI**	
29/1/53-14/2/53**LC**	New leading driving axle, driving axleboxes refitted, inside connecting rods refitted, driving springs refitted
21/9/53-17/10/53**G**	
7/12/55-7/1/56**LI-HI**	86,891; Large type diameter chimney 'similar to rebuilt MN 35018'
20/3/57-13/4/57**LI**	133,204
30/7/58-11/10/58**G**	177,210; regulator handle modified, boiler 860
18/3/60-23/3/60**LC**	53,856; frame flaw over left-hand driving horn
12/8/60-3/9/60**LI**	68,684; AWS, Regulator stuffing box and gland, speedometer

Sheds
Stewarts Lane from new
Nine Elms 10/37
Stewarts Lane 18/10/38
Nine Elms 2/12/38
Bournemouth 24/2/43
Eastleigh 8/1/49

Withdrawn 17/2/62; final mileage 1,249,831. Stored at Ashford Works 2/62 and cut up there W/E 10/3/62

30852 SIR WALTER RALEIGH at the rear of Eastleigh shed, 17 September 1949. The engine is in malachite green and, highly visible in this light, there is a bolted plate on the smokebox where the snifting valves had been. Sometimes the removal left no trace at all, which meant a piece would have been welded in. Photograph J.H. Aston.

852 SIR WALTER RALEIGH, still with its piano front, thunders round the single line loop at Petts Wood with a boat train in pre-war days. Sir Walter Raleigh, dazzling Court figure, poet and favourite of the Queen (famously spreading his cloak for her to step on) founded the first English colony in America, as well as introducing us to both potatoes and tobacco. Imprisoned by James I, he was released to seek for El Dorado but later the King, in great spite and in order to appease the Spanish, had this English hero executed. Photograph F.H. Stingemore, The Transport Treasury.

At Eastleigh on 5 August 1953, cleaned and ready in BR green; ten inch number. Photograph J.H. Aston.

30852 SIR WALTER RALEIGH at Nine Elms shed on 19 April 1958. It was as 852 that the engine suffered a bomb hit inside the very same Nine Elms shed on the night of 16 April 1941, killing a man sheltering inside the firebox. It was over a year before it could be put back into service. Eight inch number; disc inside cab warns 'boiler empty'. Photograph J.L. Stevenson, courtesy Hamish Stevenson.

Malachite green livery, and that transitional period with BR number but no tender totem, 12 March 1951. There was a period, from about the end of 1948 to summer 1949, when many locos came out with blank tenders or tanks. 30852 emerged thus in December 1948 after a full repaint in malachite green. No Lord Nelson in fact got the BR emblem until it received the dark green. Photograph The Transport Treasury.

SIR WALTER, at (inevitably) Eastleigh shed, in BR green and with second tender emblem, 23 May 1959. It has the long boiler no.860, originally on 860 LORD HAWKE, and a rebuilt Merchant Navy chimney. 'Inwardly reliable to the end' Townroe called the Nelsons. Photograph Peter Groom.

30853 SIR RICHARD GRENVILLE
To traffic 9/1928

P/E 20/1/39	Large diameter chimney with larger rim welded to the top of the stovepipe. Flaman speed recorder
P/E 20/8/40	Self trimming bunker
11/48	Snifting valves removed, renumbered 30853
9/6/53-27/6/53**HI**	
24/12/54-5/2/55**G**	252,719
6/3/57-23/3/57**HI**	79,884
1/1/58-1/3/58**NC-G**	108,298; Bulleid pattern cylinders with 10 inch piston valves
8/7/59-14/8/59**LC**	49,028
1/4/60-30/4/60**LI**	67,463; AWS, speedometer

Sheds
Stewarts Lane from new
Nine Elms 27/2/40
Bournemouth 24/2/43
Eastleigh 8/1/49

Withdrawn 3/3/62; stored at Eastleigh Works 2-3/62 and cut up there W/E 21/4/62

'The Cunarder' again, a favourite for Eastleigh Nelsons. SIR RICHARD GRENVILLE is running light with tail lamp on at St Denys on 13 August 1956. Without local knowledge, we can still assume, from the seeming lack of coal in the tender and with SIR RICHARD in back gear and a tail lamp, that the Nelson is running back to Eastleigh shed from Southampton. Photograph J. Robertson, The Transport Treasury.

853 SIR RICHARD GRENVILLE in that striking SR sage green livery at Dover – its appearance 'excellent to a degree', just as *The Railway Gazette* put it. It got malachite green early in 1939 (the tender was not modified until the following year). In a particularly crisp view we can see the painstaking lining, on the splasher over the rear bogie wheel, for instance, and the various footsteps. Sir Richard Grenville was renowned for the last stand of the *Revenge*, defeated in the Azores by the Spanish only after 24 hours of fighting. Photograph W. Hermiston, The Transport Treasury.

Though the portrait of SIR RICHARD is less than technically perfect, it's impossible to resist this on 15 August 1956 at Eastleigh shed. If I didn't know of the photographer, the renowned John Robertson, I'd conclude this was the sort of fakery the LMS got up to for CORONATION (see *The Book of*, Irwell Press). The need to combine the aircraft with the Nelson doubtless accounts for the slight 'shake' of 30853's image. Photograph J. Robertson, The Transport Treasury.

SIR RICHARD at Salisbury shed, 5 October 1957. The class was not often photographed at Salisbury in these last years. Amongst a substantial reference collection of photographs, there are certainly very few such views to be found, yet there was in fact a regular Eastleigh Lord Nelson diagram to Salisbury, thus: 6.4am Southampton Terminus to Waterloo; 10.54am Waterloo to Salisbury; 4.5pm Salisbury to Waterloo and then 11.25pm Nine Elms to Eastleigh freight. The loco will lose its 'Maunsell' front the following year. Photograph J.H. Aston.

SIR RICHARD GRENVILLE at Oxford on 22 August 1959, with Eastern Region stock bound for Bournemouth. This one was the last to get the new cylinders and had only lost the piano front – see above for instance – the previous year. Photograph Frank Hornby.

In sparkling condition, apparent even at this distance, 30853 SIR RICHARD GRENVILLE is out on the road at Redbridge on 26 June 1957, with what is probably the 2.20pm Southampton to Bournemouth slow, a connection off the Bournemouth Belle and a regular Lord Nelson job. Despite appearances, this was a star Eastleigh Nelson diagram. The engine returned on the 5.5pm Bournemouth West to Waterloo express and came back down on the 10.30pm Waterloo-Southampton Terminus. It wasn't all boat trains for the Nelsons! Photograph R.C. Riley, The Transport Treasury.

Another super Eastleigh shed portrait, as 30853, in final condition with AWS and speedometer, undergoes attention in the yard on 29 September 1961. First BR tender emblem, though 30853 had earlier run with a tender bearing the second emblem. Photograph G.W. Morrison.

30854 HOWARD OF EFFINGHAM

To traffic 10/1928

P/E 20/12/38	Flaman speed recorder, self trimming bunker
P/E 20/6/39	Large diameter chimney
P/E 16/10/46	Bullied pattern cylinders with 10inch piston valves
3/48	S prefix added to running number 854
P/E 19/5/49	Renumbered 30854, snifting valves removed
7/8/52-11/9/52	Ex-works, visit consequent on Shawford accident of 20/7/52
3/3/53-12/3/53**LC**	
29/6/54-14/8/54**G**	201,648; Exhaust injector cone
2/11/55-23/11/55**LC**	50,153
10/4/57-11/5/57**G**	84,688
9/3/59-4/4/59**LI**	68,269; Modified regulator handle, rod, stuffing box and packing
14/10/59-21/10/59**LC**	90,560; AWS
14/6/60-25/6/60**LC**	110,957

Sheds
Nine Elms from new
Stewarts Lane 6/32
Nine Elms 27/2/40
Bournemouth 24/2/43
Eastleigh 8/1/49

Withdrawn 9/9/61; stored at Eastleigh Works 9/61 and cut up there W/E 30/9/61

Left. Eastleigh, 20 May 1957. Photograph J. Robertson, The Transport Treasury.

Below. Unusual view of a Lord Nelson. Some time in the 1930s, E854 HOWARD OF EFFINGHAM a T9 and a T1 for Eastleigh works are shunted by the pilot, B4 0-4-0T No.94. Admiral Charles Howard, the 2nd Baron, Howard of Effingham, had found his Catholic faith no barrier to high office under Elizabeth. He commanded the English fleet at the time of the Armada as its Lord High Admiral and was playing bowls with Drake when news of its approach came. He later destroyed a Spanish fleet at Cadiz, in 1596.

HOWARD OF EFFINGHAM in Southern sage green at Dover in 1939. Oddly the Nelsons had sanding only to the front driving wheels – the circular filling cap can just about be seen against the light shining through that forward gap, between the front driver and the trailing bogie wheel. Photograph The Transport Treasury.

30854 HOWARD OF EFFINGHAM waits to depart Bournemouth West. The date is not known but the engine is in malachite green, black deflectors and wheels with, typically as we are discovering, blank tender. A malachite green Nelson, of course, never saw a BR emblem; it got BR dark green (and thus the emblem) late in 1951. That could just be one of the elusive wipers on the Driver's window... It was on a Bournemouth job back in 1945 that it had fallen victim to a curious accident through a misreading of the gauge glass level by the crew. An inrush of water into the firebox occurred through a fracture and as a consequence the Fireman was injured and later died. An odd feature was the blowing out of the smokebox door which struck the smoke deflector with enough force to deform it out of gauge. HOWARD OF EFFINGHAM was later to come to grief again at Shawford, falling down the embankment in July 1952. The crew scrambled out unhurt. Photograph The Transport Treasury.

Ready for the 'Britanny Express', an 08.05 boat train to Waterloo, on the quay at Southampton on 7 February 1957. The express, a seasonal morning train up and evening train down, ran for ten years from 1954 to 1964. Photograph Frank Hornby.

An amusing contrast in front ends at Eastleigh shed, 25 August 1957. Accompanying HOWARD OF EFFINGHAM are 3440 CITY OF TRURO and 2-6-0 31814. Photograph R.C. Riley, The Transport Treasury.

30855 ROBERT BLAKE
To traffic 10/1928

P/E 22/7/38	Flaman speed recorder, tender altered to self trimming
9/39	Large diameter chimney
P/E 20/8/40	Bulleid pattern cylinders with 10inch piston valves
P/E 18/5/47	Second set of Bulleid pattern cylinders
P/E 16/1/49	Renumbered 30855, snifting valves removed
9/12/52-10/1/53**Int**	
30/12/53-9/1/54**LC**	148,165; Exhaust injector cone
22/3/54-3/4/54**LC**	155,186
20/6/55-30/7/55**G**	207,873; Tyres turned, boiler 860
21/6/57-3/8/57**LI**	66,792
2/1/58-9/1/58**NC-LC**	80,018; Bogie tyres turned
26/6/58-16/8/58**G**	95,467; Regulator handle modified; standard boiler regained
27/5/60-18/6/60**HI**	58,668; AWS, speedometer

Sheds
Nine Elms from new
Stewarts Lane 6/32
Nine Elms 27/2/40
Bournemouth 24/2/43
Nine Elms 8/1/49
Eastleigh 4/2/50

Withdrawn 30/9/61; final mileage 1,239,589. Stored at Eastleigh Works 9/61-1/62 and cut up there W/E 10/2/62

Penge East and 855 ROBERT BLAKE, in original condition, passes the signal box, doubtless with another boat train. In D.W. Winkworth's memorable rendering, 'an unflattering decision' was taken in 1936 when the new 'Night Ferry' sleeper was deemed too heavy for the Nelsons. It certainly was unflattering, given that they had so memorably been intended for 500 tons at the speed of 55 mph. The authorities resorted to double heading by 4-4-0s. By 1956 *The Railway Observer* could feel able to express some surprise that a Lord Nelson, of all things, could be entrusted with the Bournemouth Belle when it was loaded to over 500 tons. They should have looked up *The Railway Gazette* account... Robert Blake was a Somerset Puritan who had once captured Taunton from the Royalists in the Civil War, a soldier who became the most celebrated seaman until Nelson's day. He defeated the Dutch off the Texel in 1653 and captured the Spanish treasure fleet at Santa Cruz de Tenerife, only to die at sea on the voyage home. Photograph F.H. Stingemore, The Transport Treasury.

ROBERT BLAKE at Eastleigh in 1949. Photograph The Transport Treasury.

ROBERT BLAKE in excellent condition, for it was fresh out of a General in the adjacent works, at Eastleigh on 12 August 1955 equipped with long boiler no. 860. Photograph J. Robertson, The Transport Treasury. *Inset.* Eastleigh, 12 August 1955. Photograph J. Robertson, The Transport Treasury.

30855 ROBERT BLAKE in the down bay at Southampton Central, 6 June 1951. Says Jim Aston: 'I took it five times, it was such a sitting bird! A half-day cheap ticket Waterloo-Southampton was available that day on the 11.30 Waterloo, part of which can be seen behind in one of the pictures. I didn't waste any time getting down on the track!' Look for the other prints in the Lord Nelson *Photographic Accompaniment...* Photographs J.H. Aston.

Stirring portrait by Peter Groom of 30855 ROBERT BLAKE on its way out of Waterloo, at Vauxhall on the 10.55am to Salisbury, 13 June 1959. The 7P power class was equivalent to Scots, A3s and others but though such engines were still happily roaring away on top services everywhere, the Nelsons by this time were increasingly second rank. Maybe it was the sheer numbers of Pacifics available on the Southern, for there were a number of trains, to Bournemouth and so on, that saw a Nelson only when a Pacific was not available. Photograph Peter Groom.

30855 ROBERT BLAKE, still game, leans into the job at Battledown, 4 September 1959. Photograph J. Robertson, The Transport Treasury.

30856 LORD St VINCENT
To traffic 11/28

P/E 23/11/38   Large diameter chimney, Flaman speed recorder
P/E 21/7/39   Multiple jet blast and large built up chimney, malachite green
P/E 21/5/40   Self trimming bunker, Bulleid pattern cylinders with 10 inch piston valves
P/E 17/3/48   Snifting valves removed, renumbered 30856
3/11/53-21/11/53**LI**
26/4/54-1/5/54**LC**   92,332; R C W Injector
16/3/55-9/4/55**HI**   132,624; R C W Injector
30/12/55-7/1/56**NC**   162,769
19/10/56-17/11/56**G**   187,417
19/9/57-20/9/57**NC**   36,567
11/9/58-4/10/58   Regulator handle modified
10/2/59-18/2/59**LC**   79,339
16/6/59-27/6/59**LC**   85,210
5/8/60-10/9/60**G**   115,700; AWS, regulator stuffing box and gland, speedometer

Sheds
Nine Elms from new
Stewarts Lane 6/32
Nine Elms 10/37
Stewarts Lane 18/10/38
Nine Elms 27/2/40
Bournemouth 31/5/48
Nine Elms 4/9/49
Eastleigh 4/2/50

Withdrawn 22/9/62; stored at Eastleigh Works 9-10/62 and cut up there W/E 17/11/62

Still in malachite but with BR 6 inch numbering and 9 inch lettering, at Waterloo platform 10 with the 6pm West of England train, 22 April 1948. Photograph J.H. Aston.

856 LORD ST VINCENT in its new malachite, at Eastleigh shed, naturally. With the Lemaître exhaust and the original cylinders (betrayed by the steam pipe and not replaced till 1940) this would be 1939. The green inside the wheel rim shows particularly well, along with the power class 'A' on the running plate. Flaman speed recorder driven from rear crank pin. First Lord of the Admiralty, 1801-1804, St Vincent led a drive to eradicate corruption in the Navy Board. Photograph The Transport Treasury.

On 19 August 1961 30856 LORD ST VINCENT runs through Hinton Admiral with a Waterloo-Bournemouth train. Photograph G.W. Morrison.

A jolly image at Eastleigh shed, 15 August 1961. The fitter, surely, is not going to get all the way down and all the way back up again, and has sent his mate to the stores for whatever part or tool he needs next. In the meantime the dome cover makes a handy foot rest. Note the pipe clipped along the running plate for the AWS receiver at the front and compare the battery box position with 30853 on page 17. Photograph G.W. Morrison.

LORD ST VINCENT at Eastleigh, 31 August 1962. It was withdrawn weeks, if not days later but it is fully coaled and lined up between two locos clearly not anywhere near withdrawal, so maybe it has a few more trips left in it. Photograph Peter Groom.

30857 LORD HOWE

To traffic 12/1928

28/1/37	Ex-works with taper boiler 1063, round top firebox
10/38	Flaman speed recorder
P/E 21/7/39	Bulleid style cylinders with 10 inch piston valves, self trimming bunker, large diameter chimney
P/E 24/7/41	Taper boiler removed, replaced by standard one with extended smokebox
13/1/43	Ex-works, taper boiler with round top firebox previously carried 28/1/37-27/9/41
W/E 7/4/45	Fitted with Belpaire boiler
P/E 20/11/49	Renumbered 30857; snifting valves removed
30/5/52-4/7/52**G**	
26/2/53-27/3/53**HC**	
8/12/53-31/12/53**LI**	
22/3/54-27/3/54**NC-LC**	74,173; exhaust injector cones, boiler patch plates
6/10/54-23/10/54**LC**	106,302
11/8/55-10/9/55**G**	133,805
1/2/57-2/3/57**LC**	55,549
22/9/58-18/10/58**HI**	65,124; regulator handle modified
1/6/60-30/7/60**G**	123,050; AWS, speedometer, regulator stuffing box and gland
22/5/62-26/5/62**NC**	

Sheds
Nine Elms from new
Stewarts Lane 6/32
Nine Elms 6/33
Stewarts Lane 13/11/37
Nine Elms 27/2/40
Eastleigh 4/2/50

Withdrawn 22/9/62; stored at Eastleigh Works 9/62 and cut up there W/E 20/10/62

Left. A close up of LORD HOWE at Salisbury, with the taper boiler. Note how lining runs around lower extension of nameplate. Photograph The Transport Treasury.

Below. 857 LORD HOWE in its original guise; this is Dover, at a guess. Lamp irons have been moved 'inboard' in response to the fitting of smoke deflectors. A reforming First Lord of the Admiralty, Howe restored to prowess a run-down and neglected Navy in the 1780s. Photograph The Transport Treasury.

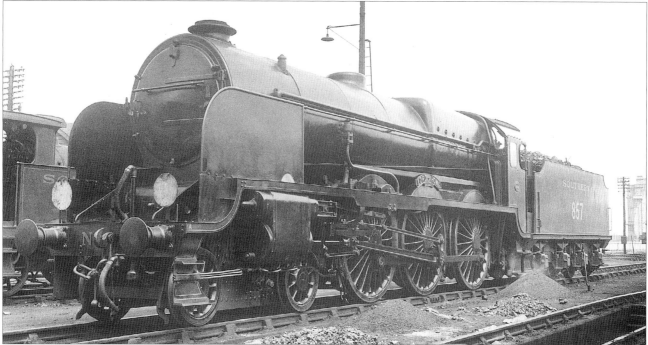

LORD HOWE as it looked with the taper boiler – very different indeed. This is Salisbury shed, so the year would probably be 1937; LORD HOWE carried the boiler first from January that year and was at Nine Elms working the Western Section for nearly a year, going to Stewarts Lane at the end of 1937. The boiler was removed in the autumn of 1941 and though it was borne again by LORD HOWE from January 1943 to February 1945, for this latter period it wore black livery. It was tried out on Dover boat trains where it steamed more freely than the conventionally equipped Nelsons, 'except when the engines had to be driven hard' according to Townroe. 'Clearly' he writes, 'the draughting was wrong and further experiments were needed with the blastpipe and chimney'. The enthusiasm for this investigative work was not forthcoming and Maunsell retired the following year. Photograph The Transport Treasury.

LORD HOWE with Pullmans – the location defeats me and only hopeless naiveté leads to the assumption it is the Golden Arrow – but at least the discs look right. Whatever the particular working here, the Lord Nelsons had handled the 'Arrow' from the first; indeed it was later the reason four of them got the 'Dover' green – to match the coaches used with the Pullmans. The War ended the Arrow of course and the Nelsons never reappeared on it. LORD HOWE has the newly acquired smoke deflectors – note how lamp irons still project from smokebox rim.

Platform 10 at Waterloo (see Jim Aston's 30856 in the previous section) and the 6pm West of England train again; this is 22 April 1948, a month earlier than the view of 30856, and the new numbers have yet to appear. Scintillating malachite livery; Nine Elms had kept the engine in superb condition ever since it worked the Royal Wedding Special (Princess Elizabeth and Prince Philip) the previous year. Photograph J.H. Aston.

LORD HOWE shunting the stock yard at Clapham Junction on 25 April 1954. A gorgeous study showing often obscure detail of the boiler top and roof, stowed fire irons and so on, though the elusive front sand filler cap maintains it customary invisibility. BR green, 'A' power class, 10 inch numerals and first BR tender emblem. This was the small version – 30857 was the only Lord Nelson to get it. Photograph R. Wilson, The Transport Treasury.

LORD HOWE with second tender emblem at Nine Elms on 21 May 1957 and now with eight inch numbers. The tenders frequently bore that 'knocked about' look, due no doubt to movement in the internal joins and welds made on their enlargement years before. LORD HOWE seems to have suffered one of those 'slow motion scrapes' in to the bargain. Photograph J. Robertson, The Transport Treasury.

30858 LORD DUNCAN
To traffic 1/1929

P/E 24/2/38	Monitor live steam injector
P/E 21/4/39	Large diameter chimney, Flaman speed recorder
P/E 21/5/40	Speed recorder removed, self trimming bunker
P/E 13/2/48	Snifting valves removed
P/E 13/6/48	Renumbered 30858
7/10/49	Derailed in Southampton Docks and sent to Eastleigh Works
P/E 19/1/51	Bulleid pattern cylinders with 10 inch piston valves
17/10/52-22/11/52**NC**	
6/8/53-14/8/53**LC**	
30/7/54-21/8/54**LI**	111,812; boiler barrel plates
14/4/55-1/5/55**LC**	At Nine Elms
16/11/56-15/12/56**G**	187,119
4/7/58-10/7/58**LC**	61,823; regulator handle modified
15/9/58-20/9/58**LC**	68,103
5/10/58-10/10/58**NC**	88,614
26/6/59-1/8/59**HI**	85,145; regulator stuffing box and gland modified
5/10/59-10/10/59**NC**	AWS
19/8/60-3/9/60**LC**	124,385

Sheds
Stewarts Lane from new
Nine Elms 9/12/38
Eastleigh 6/6/58

Withdrawn 19/8/61; stored at Eastleigh Works 8-10/61 and cut up there W/E 25/11/61

Apparently ex-works after light repair in April 1949, a nonetheless rather tired LORD DUNCAN, at Nine Elms. Duncan saved England from invasion by the Dutch twice in 1797, despite the Navy being plagued by mutiny. He daringly fooled the enemy into staying in port by using false signals and, later in the year, destroyed the Dutch fleet at Camperdown. Photograph Canon George, The Transport Treasury.

In markedly better form, at Nine Elms again and now in BR green, 21 May 1957. Photograph J. Robertson, The Transport Treasury.

With the familiar tender dints and warps, LORD DUNCAN stands in lovely condition at Eastleigh on 23 May 1959. Water treatment symbol under number. Photograph Peter Groom.

A very different story at Eastleigh, 15 August 1961. The end is nigh for LORD DUNCAN, you must fear, for its withdrawal is recorded that very month. Despite that healthy tender-full of good quality coal it's the torch for 30858. In a way it is slightly surprising the Nelsons lasted as long as they did. As Townroe almost shockingly points out, they were obsolescent even in 1948 'and quite obsolescent alongside the excellent BR Class 5s, easily serviced and maintained'. In theory, the generous pool of Pacifics meant that: 'there was, on paper, little justification for keeping so many Arthurs and Nelsons but the number of Pacifics available for service on any given day fluctuated widely, and the Maunsell engines had to be held in reserve to make up deficiencies'. This tender was one of four Lord Nelson tenders that never acquired the later BR emblem. Photograph G.W. Morrison.

30859 LORD HOOD
To traffic 3/1929

P/E 21/10/38	Flaman speed recorderr
P/E 19/5/39	Large diameter chimney
W/E 21/1/40	Ex-works with high sided tender
P/E 17/11/46	Bulleid pattern cylinders with 10 inch piston valves
P/E 13/2/48	Snifting valves removed
P/E 20/2/49	Renumbered 30859
24/9/52-18/10/52**Int**	
9/6/53-20/6/53**LC**	
2/10/53-24/10/53**LI**	
19/4/55-21/5/55**G**	176,914; exhaust injector cone [Examined]
30/1/56-10/2/56**LC**	31,846 standard exam. only
14/2/57-9/3/57**LI**	68,413
18/3/58-12/4/58**LI**	107,012
20/8/59-19/9/59**G**	156,892; AWS, regulator handle modified, regulator stuffing box and gland
5/3/61-25/3/61**LC**	46,209

Sheds
Stewarts Lane from new
Nine Elms 27/2/40
Eastleigh 6/6/58

Withdrawn 9/12/62; stored at Eastleigh Works 10-11/61 and cut up there W/E 23/12/61

LORD HOOD on the turntable at Nine Elms, its home shed since 1940, 17 August 1951. Quite markedly different by now (see above opposite) with Lemaître exhaust, high tender, flat front, lamp irons on smokebox door, snifting valves gone, and so on. Photograph J. Robertson, The Transport Treasury.

859 LORD HOOD in its first days; from the maritime background this is presumably Dover. Certainly the engine was at Stewarts Lane for its first decade or so, so this is unlikely to be Southampton. Front lamp irons have not gone 'inboard' yet. Urie 5,000 gallon tender with curved top. A famous Navy name – Lord Hood was born a vicar's son; he commanded the *Barfluer* in the Caribbean and became a Lord of the Admiralty in 1788. Nelson served under him and his Trafalgar battle plan is said to have been inspired in part by a plan of Hood's to attack the French at anchor in the Mediterranean.

30859 LORD HOOD near Southampton Terminus with an Ocean Liner Express for the Greek Line ship 'Neptune', 26 June 1957. Photograph R.C. Riley, The Transport Treasury.

LORD HOOD at Southampton on 11 October 1958. A couple of years earlier, on Sunday 29 January 1956, 30859 had been the first (the only?) Nelson on record to work a passenger train over the Brighton line on a Sunday. With the crew doubtless oblivious to this admittedly-obscure claim to fame, LORD HOOD was used on 4.45am London Bridge-Brighton. 30859 had been filched, apparently, on its way to works and accordingly, *The Railway Observer* relates, 30859 'had given its unaccustomed Bricklayers Arms crew a somewhat rough ride'. Photograph R.C. Riley, The Transport Treasury.

LORD HOOD of course, was the Nelson with the smaller driving wheels though it is hard to see the four inch deficiency in any but a smack-bang side view, which of course we don't have. You can *almost* convince yourself... 30859 is standing, inevitably, at Eastleigh shed, on 23 May 1959. Photograph Peter Groom.

30860 LORD HAWKE

To traffic 4/1929

11/36	Fitted with Standard LN boiler. Regained long boiler no.860
at next visit (9/37)	
P/E 21/7/39	Bulleid pattern cylinders with 10 inch piston valves, large diameter chimney, Flaman speed recorder, self trimming bunker
P/E 15/8/48	Renumbered 30860, snifting valves removed
14/4/53-5/5/53**LI**	
4/2/55-12/3/55**G**	147,089; exhaust injector cone; standard boiler
25/10/56-17/11/56**LI**	70,906
12/3/58-15/3/58**LC**	49,453
13/10/58-1/11/58**LI**	137,815; regulator handle modified
27/6/60-9/7/60**LC**	188,446
2/11/60-17/12/60**G**	199,480; AWS, regulator stuffing box and gland, speedometer
22-23/12/61**NC**	

Sheds
Stewarts Lane from new
Nine Elms 6/32
Bournemouth 6/6/58
Eastleigh 26/11/59

Withdrawn 11/8/62; final mileage 1,367,841. Stored at Eastleigh Works 8/62 and cut up there W/E 1/9/62

LORD HAWKE awaiting departure at Brookwood, about 1952. As Winkworth points out, the end of the war certainly saw a profound change in the circumstances of the class. In 1939 the Nelsons had been the front line, on a rising tide of solid improvement. Come the peace the Merchant Navy Pacifics were in charge of the top duties while everything else was falling to the incoming light Pacifics. Photograph The Transport Treasury.

860 LORD HAWKE, as built without smoke deflectors, at Nine Elms. It was the last of the first batch of ten; the succeeding batch of five, 861-865, had the deflectors from new. With the longer boiler, there is no 'piano' front. Yet another Admiral to deflect foreign invasion, Hawke hurled his ships into battle in appalling conditions with the legendary cry 'Lay me alongside the French Admiral/the *Soleil Royale*' (accounts vary). The Brest fleet which was to cover the invasion barges was destroyed at Quiberon Bay in November 1759 and Hawke was duly and rightly acclaimed a national hero. The Photograph F.H. Stingemore.

We are back to Jim Aston's Platform 10 at Waterloo again, and the 6pm West of England train, this time on 22 June 1949. Grubby malachite green and BR numbering/lettering. The skeletal Waterloo roof still awaits its glass, blown out and then cleared away during the war. Photograph J.H. Aston.

The photographers would be out on a summer Saturday... First we have a train from Bournemouth to the Midlands running into Basingstoke behind LORD HAWKE on 22 August 1959, a typical summer Saturday working for a Lord Nelson. That day LORD HAWKE ran to the Nelsons' northern outpost, Oxford, where it turned at the shed ready for return to the south coast. As the Navy meets the Air Force, 30860 duly waits to take over the return from a Castle, 5071 SPITFIRE. By this time 30860 had a standard LN boiler. Photographs Frank Hornby and N.L. Browne, John Stretton Collection.

LORD HAWKE at Battledown, 4 September 1959. Photograph J. Robertson, The Transport Treasury.

LORD HAWKE, with that sort of slumped look, at Eastleigh on Saturday 4 August 1962, with all the latest fitments – AWS plus cab holes, speedometer, conduit along valence. It was withdrawn that very month (it may already be in store – it doesn't exactly look like it's been thrown into the fray of summer Saturday working) and cut up a few weeks later. Condemned engines did not hang around then. Photograph G.W. Morrison.

30861 LORD ANSON
To traffic 9/1929

P/E 22/9/38	Large diameter chimney, Flaman speed recorder, self trimming bunker
P/E 24/5/43	Bulleid pattern cylinders with 10 inch piston valves
P/E 19/11/47	Snifting valves removed, repainted malachite green to haul a Royal train [replaced by No.857]
29/4/52-7/6/52**G**	
11/12/52-28/1/53**NC**	
6/8/54-11/9/54**G**	101,652; W/E 4/9/54, 'awaiting boiler'
12/3/56-13/4/56**LI**	77,261
25/9/56-6/10/56**LC**	
23/4/57-3/5/57**NC**	113,448
30/1-22/2/58**LI-HI**	141,586
1/9/58-6/9/58**LC**	162,636
17/11/59-12/12/59**G**	202,642; regulator handle modified, speedometer, regulator stuffing box and packing
24/3/60-2/4/60**LC**	2,196; AWS
3/1/62-27/1/62**LC**	71,175

Sheds
Stewarts Lane from new
Nine Elms 6/32
Stewarts Lane 2/12/38
Nine Elms 27/2/40
Bournemouth 31/5/48
Nine Elms 4/9/49
Eastleigh 5/6/56

Withdrawn 6/10/62, stored at Eastleigh Works 9-10/62 and cut up there W/E 24/11/62

Stovepipe chimneyed LORD ANSON at an unknown location, though it could be Ashford. This was the Lord Nelson which went to the Liverpool & Manchester celebrations in 1930 in the guise of LORD NELSON. This is the livery applied to some of the stovepipe chimney engines that were being experimented with in the late 1930s. There were four of them, 855, 856, 861 and 863, decked out in olive green, cream and dark green lining, plain black cylinders and smoke deflectors with nine inch gilt and shadow number and nine inch SOUTHERN on the tender. Admiral Sir George Anson's flotilla made a famous cruise round the world in 1740-44. Most of his men were lost to scurvy and he returned with just one ship, but with £1,250,000-worth of plunder. Anson developed the 'general chase' and demonstrated its devastating power by demolishing a French Squadron off Cape Finisterre in 1747.

Oxford again, 2 April 1956. This is the north end, so 30861 LORD ANSON has arrived from Bournemouth and is now moving forward to let the WR engine take over. Photograph R.C. Riley, The Transport Treasury.

LORD ANSON in BR green, 20 May 1957. The location, inevitably, is Eastleigh shed. This particular Nelson had figured in coal consumption trials under Bulleid in 1946, along with 21C14 NEDERLAND LINE and 789 SIR GUY. LORD ANSON returned a little under 45lbs per mile, which was hardly remarkable, for it was what was expected of a Nelson at the time (Winkworth). Such figures are what you make of them of course, and Bradley uses the same figure to make a fascinating historical point, given the associations of the Lord Nelson design with that of the Royal Scots – LORD ANSON's figures were almost exactly comparable to the LM's 46154 THE HUSSAR in the BR locomotive exchanges eighteen months or so later. Photograph J. Robertson, The Transport Treasury.

Eastleigh station 13 May 1958, and the 2pm to Bournemouth. Photograph Brian Morrison.

LORD ANSON in its last summer, in its last weeks of work, but still pretty as a picture, 31 August 1962. Photograph Peter Groom.

30862 LORD COLLINGWOOD

To traffic 10/1929

8/34	Kylchap exhaust, double chimney
P/E 22/9/38	Flaman speed recorder
P/E 19/5/39	Large diameter chimney
P/E 31/12/39	Bulleid type cylinders with 10 inch piston valves, extended smokebox, self trimming bunker
30/6/48-7/8/48**G**	124,603; renumbered 30862, snifting valves removed
26/9/52-25/10/52**Int**	
8/2/54-6/3/54**G**	144,513; exhaust injector cone
16/11/55-10/12/55**LI**	89,608
23/4/57-27/4/57**LC**	137,551
5/5/58-7/6/58**G**	169,052
29/7/58-9/8/58**LC**	5,438
21/4/61-13/5/61**HI**	89,940; AWS, regulator stuffing box gland and packing, speedometer

Sheds
Stewarts Lane from new
Nine Elms 6/32
Stewarts Lane 10/37
Nine Elms 18/10/38
Bournemouth 6/45
Nine Elms 31/5/48
Bournemouth 4/9/49
Eastleigh 5/6/56

Withdrawn 6/10/62, stored at Eastleigh Works 10/61 and cut up there W/E 27/10/62
Said to be highest Nelson mileage at 1,390,329

862 LORD COLLINGWOOD with its new double chimney fitted a few weeks before, on the turntable at Nine Elms on 15 September 1934; the conditions have picked out the colder water tank of the tender in a sheet of condensation. Collingwood on the *Royal Sovereign* had taken over from Nelson when the Rear Admiral was shot at Trafalgar. He was notable among other feats for strolling the deck of his ship munching on an apple as red hot iron poured into it. The *Royal Sovereign* had been the first ship to engage the French and Spanish Combined Fleet at Trafalgar. Photograph H.C. Casserley, courtesy R.M. Casserley.

Oxford again, with LORD COLLINGWOOD ready to return south, 6 June 1951. Photograph The Transport Treasury.

Every class did its share of filling in on empty stock and so on as part of everyday diagrams but (this is far from scientifically precise) examining photo collections tends to throw up many more instances of Nelsons on ECS, locals, shunting (even propelling stock through the washer at Bournemouth West) as, say, the Merchant Navys. Take LORD COLLINGWOOD at Bournemouth Central on 11 June 1953, running through with, of all things, a pick-up freight. The auxiliary vacuum reservoirs show up well, together with the interconnecting pipe. Photograph The Transport Treasury.

30862 LORD COLLINGWOOD near Southampton Central with the 12.35pm from Waterloo, 7 November 1959. Photograph D.W. Winkworth.

The sublime and the ridiculous. LORD COLLINGWOOD takes American *artiste* Liberace ('AND GEORGE TOO!') and entourage up to London on 25 September 1956. Photograph S.C. Nash.

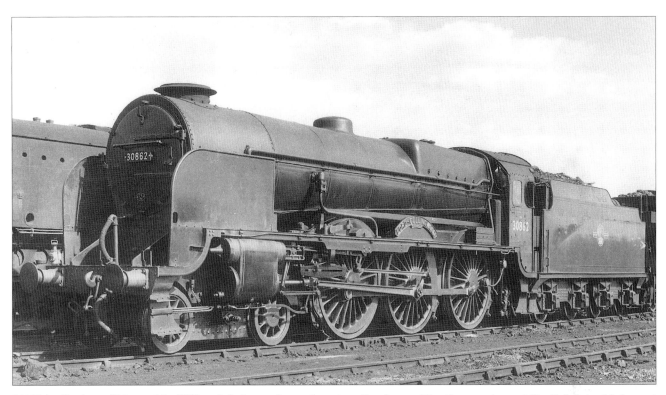

30862 in final condition with AWS, cab holes and speedometer, lined up with other engines at Eastleigh on 17 August 1961. It was withdrawn along with 30861 in October the following year; these were the last two Nelsons to go. All the Nelsons finished up at Eastleigh, as we know, under Stephen Townroe who was in charge of the shed there and although he could be critical of the Nelsons he was in fact proud to have them on the Eastleigh books (he later came to possess the nameplate LORD COLLINGWOOD – the 'C' in S.C. Townroe stood for Collingwood!). He didn't want Pacifics for 'the boats' (as they were called) because they couldn't be kept quiet and smoke-free in the Docks. Nine Elms weren't so fussy and freely used light Pacifics on such jobs. Photograph G.W. Morrison.

30863 LORD RODNEY
To traffic 10/1929

P/E 20/5/38	Experimental large diameter chimney, Flaman speed recorder
6/39	Large diameter chimney
P/E 19/11/47	Snifting valves removed
20/7/49-16/8/49**G**	Renumbered 30863
29/9/51-2/11/51**HI**	
5/5/53-22/5/53**LC**	
14/1/54-23/1/54**LC**	198,130
21/5/54-26/6/54**G**	208,923
13/12/55-14/1/56**LI**	72,468
28/8/56-15/9/56**LC**	99,862; left-hand cylinder renewed
19/10/56-3/11/56**LC**	101,991; collision damage, front end renewed
30/8/57-28/8/57**G**	129,454
20/12/57-9/1/58**NC**	4,867; Three way steam pipe casting renewed
12/6/58-27/6/58**LC**	52,578; left-hand steam pipe castings and pipes repaired and refitted
9/10/59-15/10/59**NC**	60,358; AWS
21/1/60-29/1/60**NC**	67,998
1/2/61-10/3/61**HC**	97,181

Sheds
Stewarts Lane from new
Nine Elms 18/10/38
Stewarts Lane 2/12/38
Nine Elms 27/2/40
Bournemouth 6/45
Nine Elms 31/5/48
Bournemouth 4/9/49
Eastleigh 5/6/56

Withdrawn 10/2/62, stored at Ashford Works 2/62 and cut up there W/E 24/2/62

Boat train working with 863. LORD RODNEY has the later style of 'No', that is with a dot beneath the line. It came in after the abolition of the 'E' prefix and is seemingly impossible to represent on modern type setting! Admiral George Rodney, with the injunction from Admiralty 'the fate of the Empire is in your hands' in 1782 ejected the French from the West Indies using the new and devastating 'carronades' cast at the Falkirk Ironworks – a powerful indication of Britain's growing industrial dominance.

30863 ex-works at the rear of Eastleigh shed, 20 August 1949. The lining nicely follows the contour of the valance of the running plate. Only the first five Nelsons turned out in the BR dark green were thus favoured. Penny pinching afterwards meant the lining – 'economy' lining – went straight along. Photograph J.H. Aston.

LORD RODNEY at Brockenhurst on 2 May 1953. Photograph R.C. Riley, The Transport Treasury.

Up passenger train leaving Basingstoke in a trail of smoke behind 30863 LORD RODNEY, 24 June 1956. Photograph R.C. Riley, The Transport Treasury.

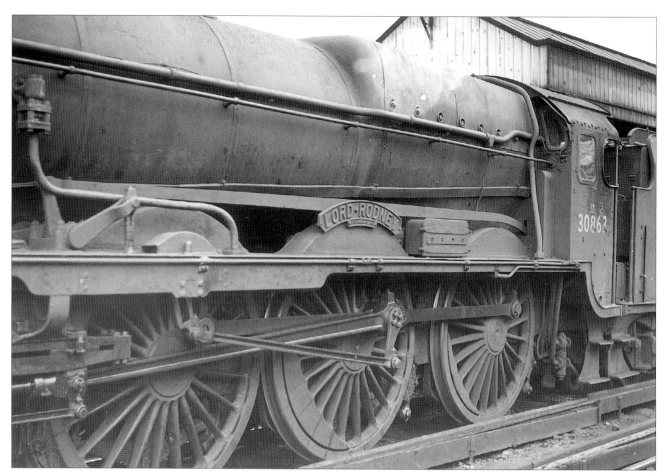

A good close-up of some Lord Nelson detail. The 'mini' splasher adjacent to the front splasher, a hinged cover for inspection and lubrication, shows well. The open end was a hand hold to raise it open – it was hinged at the cab-ward end. Photograph Nigel Lester, The Transport Treasury.

LORD RODNEY at Nine Elms on 23 March 1956; this is the one that kept its Maunsell cylinders, hence the 'piano' front between the frames below the smokebox door. The older south London terraces sweeping away to a new tower block indicate something of the changing face of the district. Photograph Peter Groom.

The last journey of LORD RODNEY – passing Knockholt on 3 February 1962. This was an engineer's train from Hither Green to Tonbridge, a working which was utilised to get the engine on its way to Ashford for scrapping. It seemed a bit distasteful, really... Protection plate behind coupling, fitted in conjunction with AWS equipment. Photograph S.C. Nash.

30864 SIR MARTIN FROBISHER

To traffic 11/1929

P/E 21/10/38	Flaman speed recorder, self trimming bunker
P/E 20/6/39	Standard large diameter chimney
P/E 17/3/48	Bulleid pattern cylinders with 10 inch piston valves, snifting valves removed, renumbered 0864
5/3/53-8/3/53**LI**	
14/1/54-23/1/54**LC**	137,876; R C W injector
3/12/54-24/12/54**LI**	184,655
15/6/56-14/7/56**G**	246,564
14/10/57-9/11/57**LI**	47,796
11/4/58-19/4/58**LC**	56,243
1/10/59-31/10/59**LI**	93,356; AWS, regulator handle modified, regulator stuffing box, gland and packing

Sheds
Stewarts Lane from new
Nine Elms 13/11/37
Bournemouth 6/45
Dorchester 13/5/54
Bournemouth 31/10/54
Eastleigh 26/11/59

Withdrawn 27/1/62, stored at Eastleigh Works 1-2/62 and cut up there W/E 10/3/62

30864 SIR MARTIN FROBISHER out on the road at Radipole Halt on the Weymouth line, with what is probably the Weymouth portion of a Waterloo train. Photograph The Transport Treasury.

Beautiful in malachite green, 864 SIR MARTIN FROBISHER shows off that wonderful boiler. This is presumably 1939, when the engine first got this livery, along with the Lemaître exhaust. When malachite appeared again, after the war, the paintwork did not include the footsteps (as visible here). The pattern of studs on the right-hand cabside indicates equipment fixed inside for the Flaman recorder. No wonder the Armada was defeated; the first four ships shadowing the Spanish up the Channel were commanded, in order, by Howard, Drake, Hawkins and Frobisher. The English could manoeuvre as they liked while, with a strong south-westerly blowing, the Spanish could not turn. Photograph The Transport Treasury.

30864 SIR MARTIN FROBISHER looking very much down in the mouth, on the Eastleigh 'dump' awaiting the call to works, 14 May 1949. It was one of three that had got the ill-fated apple green the previous year; it weathered poorly, as we can see, but nevertheless survived the works visit. The only change when it was ex-works in June was that BRITISH RAILWAYS was painted out and the SR style numbers replaced by Gill Sans. The next change was BR dark green in 1951. Photograph J.H. Aston.

SIR MARTIN passing Loco Junction, Nine Elms, on 6 September 1958. The Nelsons were only ever to be found at a handful of sheds – restricted even further after they left Stewarts Lane to spend the rest of their years at Eastleigh, Bournemouth and Nine Elms. The exception was Dorchester and two, 30864 and 30865, spent a few months there in 1954. Photograph R.C. Riley, The Transport Treasury.

Near the end, at the Eastleigh coaling stage on 13 August 1961. Another example of the first tender emblem surviving to the bitter end. Photograph G.W. Morrison.

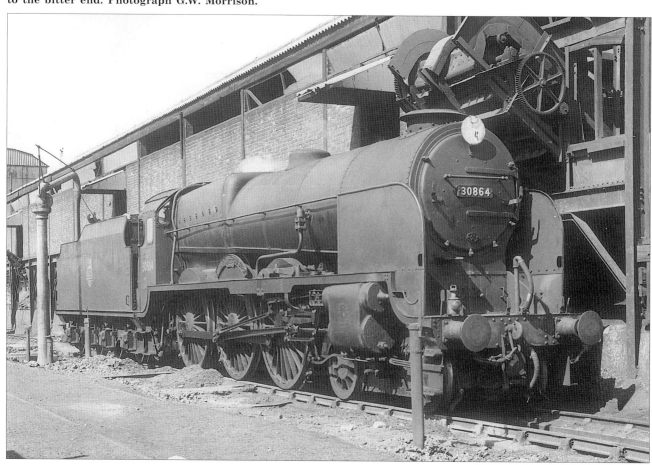

30865 SIR JOHN HAWKINS

To traffic 11/1929

P/E 24/2/38	Large diameter chimney
3/38	Kylchap exhaust, double chimney
P/E 20/6/39	Flaman speed recorder, large diameter chimney
P/E 21/6/40	Bulleid pattern cylinders with 10 inch piston valves, tender modified
P/E 13/7/48	Renumbered 30865, snifting valves removed
20/10/52-25/10/52**Casual**	
11/2/53-14/3/53**G**	
3/2/54-20/3/54**LC-LI-HI**	46,158; W/E 6/3/54 awaiting cylinders, R C W injector, tender 1012
22/12/55-28/1/56**G**	131,275; boiler barrel plates
5/7/57-17/8/57**HI**	63,575
10/2/59-28/2/59**LI**	109,411; modified regulator handle

Sheds
Stewarts Lane from new
Nine Elms 6/32
Stewarts Lane 1/10/37
Nine Elms 13/11/37
Bournemouth 26/4/45
Dorchester 13/5/54
Bournemouth 31/10/54
Eastleigh 26/11/59

Withdrawn 30/5/61, stored at Eastleigh Works 5-7/61 and cut up there W/E 2/9/61

865 SIR JOHN HAWKINS with a boat train in the 1930s, when the Nelsons were still in the front line of passenger working. 'Jack' Hawkins was Drake's cousin but his star has waned somewhat in recent years through an association with the foundation of the slave trade. Hawkins was, however, one of the most important figures in saving England from the Spanish. Not only was he in one of the leading ships shadowing the Armada up the Channel, but the old pirate had been in charge of the development of the Navy, furnishing it with fighting machines technologically superior to those of the enemy.

30865 SIR JOHN HAWKINS with a train at St Denys, 13 August 1956. Now with final cylinders and 'flat' front. Photograph J. Robertson, The Transport Treasury.

30865 SIR JOHN HAWKINS in Clapham cutting, 2 March 1957. A clue to the longevity of the class comes the peak nature of much of the work on the Southern. The Western Section in theory was amply provided for with respect to express power, with Pacifics and King Arthurs but on summer Saturdays even this was not enough, and all the 'lesser' 4-6-0s were thrown into the fray. Photograph R.C. Riley, The Transport Treasury.

SIR JOHN resplendent at Waterloo, 29 September 1951, displaying some fine front end detail. The later angular steam pipes can just be made out. H.S. Brighty, The Transport Treasury.

Inset. Nine Elms 17 August 1956. The tender finished up behind Schools 4-4-0 30912 DOWNSIDE. Photograph J. Robertson, The Transport Treasury.

APPENDICES

Appendix 1

FROM *THE RAILWAY GAZETTE*,
November 5th, 1926
'FOUR-CYLINDER 4-6-0 TYPE
EXPRESS ENGINES ON THE
GREAT WESTERN AND
SOUTHERN RAILWAYS
'A brief Analysis of Two Designs,
each of which has in turn been
characterised as the most Powerful
Passenger Locomotive in Great
Britain'

The 4-6-0 wheel arrangement has for several years past been employed in connection with express passenger service on railways in the United Kingdom, the type having in many ways proved the most satisfactory that can be used to meet the traffic conditions imposed. The particular grouping of wheels referred to is associated in this, as in other countries, with varying cylinder dispositions, and, in fact, all the customary cylinder arrangements have been combined with it. Thus, we have two-cylinder 4-6-0 type locomotives, some with inside and others with outside cylinders, and others again with three and four cylinders, non-compound in all cases. There is, therefore, no lack of opportunity for preparing comparative data on a wide scale if these were needed.

'It is not, however, intended in the present article to cover a scope of this magnitude, but to limit our remarks to a comparison of the two engines for which the claim of being the most powerful passenger locomotive in Great Britain has been consecutively put forward.

'The engines referred to are those of the 'Castle' class on the Great Western, designed by Mr C.B. Collett, Chief Mechanical Engineer and built at the Swindon Works and the more recent Lord Nelson locomotive, designed by Mr R.E.L. Maunsell, Chief Mechanical Engineer of the Southern Railway.

'The first of the 'Castle' engines, namely the Caerphilly Castle, was introduced towards the end of 1923, since which time several others of the same design have been built and put into service. These engines are a development of the well-known 'Star' class on the Great Western Railway, and when first brought out it was claimed that this was the most powerful express passenger engine in Great Britain, the basis of computation being that of the tractive force developed. This is commonly accepted as a means by which locomotive power shall be measured, but, as was stated on a previous occasion, it does not always prove that an engine, figuratively superior

to another in this respect, ranks above it in point of capacity for effective work in starting and hauling heavy trains.

'It is doubtless, as generally thought, that some better power definition for locomotives is now called for, but as the claims made for both the Great Western engine and that of the Southern Railway are based in each case upon the figures relating to tractive force, it will suffice for the present to utilise that factor in the comparison to be made.

'In both cases the design is based primarily upon the objective of providing a class of engine to which can safely be entrusted the haulage of the heaviest passenger trains running on fast schedules in the most important services of the owning company and to feel that in utilising such engines there is a margin of a substantial kind to meet contingencies which normally are not identified with the running of the trains. In other words, the engines possess a sufficiency of latent power to enable them to cope on occasions with extra train loadings and still maintain punctual running, while adverse weather conditions and such like hindrances to progress are overcome by calling up in the necessary degree the reserve power in hand to meet such contingencies. This reserve may best be expressed in terms of boiler capacity and the corresponding ability it affords of working at extended cut-offs in the cylinders. Many an otherwise admirable class of locomotive such as can be relied upon to give every satisfaction in normal circumstances fails when other and more stringent duties are imposed upon it, and therefore on a big trunk railway system there is always work for the generally similar but really superior class of locomotive possessing the reserve of power that is lacking in the other.

The 'Castles' and the 'Lord Nelsons'
'The new engines, which we now proceed to compare with one another, both belong to the 'reserve power' category in the fullest sense. In several of its leading features the new Southern engine Lord Nelson is strikingly similar to the well-known 'Castle' class on the Great Western, and it is of interest to draw attention to those characteristics which are common to both designs. To commence with, both are of the now familiar 10-wheel type having the 4-6-0 wheel formation, and each design further marks the practical limit in capacity, due mainly to the fact that boilers of larger size cannot be used *[the Kings showed otherwise!]* with the wheel grouping employed.

'So far as maximum tractive effort is concerned, the engine built by Mr

Maunsell is the more powerful of the two, the figure in its case being 33,500lb as against 31,626lb for the Great Western locomotive. Ultimately, however, the actual work possible on the tender drawbar is determined by the steaming power of the boiler and the total moving weight of the engine; therefore, reference is required to these factors before computations as to the actual power at speed are attempted.

'Constructionally, these two engines are alike, and attention is directed to the four cylinders, of almost equal volume, with which each is fitted. The drive, too, is divided, the two inside cylinders being connected to the leading coupled axle, while those outside transmit their driving force to the middle axle. The Southern engine has its cylinders almost in line under the smokebox. In passing, it may be remarked that in this respect it is like the 'Lord Farringdon' class on the LNER. The GW engine, on the other hand, has the outside cylinders placed farther back and those between the frames well forward – a plan which, perhaps, complicates the pipe connections but certainly makes it possible to obtain equal connecting-rod lengths, a desirable feature for four-cylinder engines which claim the properties of close balancing.

'In the matter of crank arrangements, Mr Maunsell makes a departure in using the 135 degree arrangement, the advantage being a very equal torque, whereas with four cranks, as used generally, the turning moment is no better than that obtained with two at right angles. The GW engines belong to this latter classification. The advantages offered by the Maunsell plan, which is by no means a new one, are offset to some extent by the two extra valve gears used. They are, however, not really necessary, though probably it is expedient to adopt this plan. Further, in considering the properties of a smooth torque, while admitting the desirability of this feature, in practice its great value lies in the fact that it allows of a high tractive effort being associated with a relatively low adhesive weight, meaning a low adhesive factor. Another claim made on behalf of the crank disposition employed in this engine is that owing to there being eight separate impulses or 'beats' per revolution of the driving wheels the effect of the draught upon the fire is more uniform, giving improved combustion of fuel and more thorough heat transference.

'Referring again to the question of power, a glance at the boilers shows them to be very much alike in their leading features. The table of dimensions gives all the ratios required in order to obtain information as to

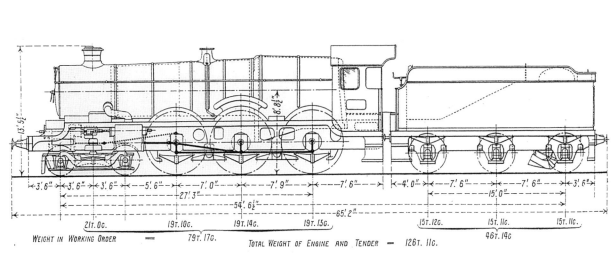

Outline Drawing of "Castle" Class Locomotive, Great Western Railway.

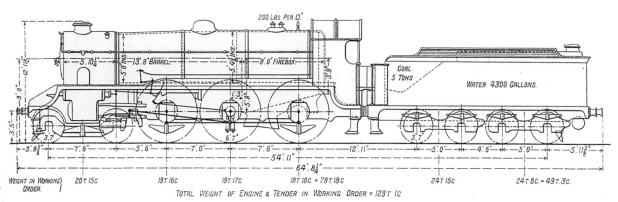

Outline Drawing of "King Arthur" Class Locomotive, Southern Railway.

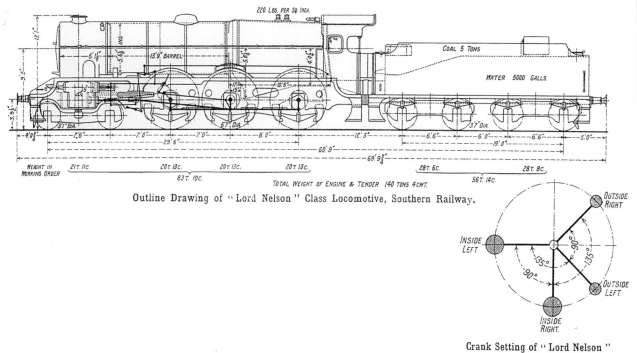

Outline Drawing of "Lord Nelson" Class Locomotive, Southern Railway.

Crank Setting of "Lord Nelson" Locomotive.

relative capacities. The boiler demand factors indicate that both designers expect much from the heating surfaces, even allowing for the low value of the combustion factors, 71.7 and 76.4 respectively. High-grade fuel accounts for this.

'Mr Maunsell's engine has a splendid firebox, and he has done well to get a firebox-grate factor of 5.88, in view of the form of box employed with its large, narrow grate. There is little, however, to choose between the two boilers, and indeed on general grounds that used for the 'King Arthur' class appeals to us the most strongly; we especially like the relationships between the power of the engines and that of the boiler. In each case the tubes are short for the sizes used, but there is something to be said for this as it means free steaming with a minimum draught.

'On the question of weight, the new Southern locomotive is heavy; a good average weight of 4-6-0 type engines run close to 76lb per square foot of combined heating surface. The engine weight and that of the tender, which must carry a large supply of water, detracts from the drawbar pull at speed, and our view is that at 60mph the GW engine and the Southern are on equal terms. The question of blast action might be discussed further, but at equal powers a possible advantage offered by Mr Maunsell's engine may be discounted by the relative power demand factors.

'The comparative tables which follow, giving the leading particulars of the Southern Railway's King Arthur and Lord Nelson locomotives and those of the Great Western Castle engine, and also some estimated data covering the principal ratios of each design, will serve further to demonstrate the leading characteristics of the respective locomotives.

'The figures right show that, while in many respects there is a marked similarity between the engines, in others they differ quite considerably, and, as shown, it is a case of weighing the points of one design against another and studying the variants which apply to each, so that a correct idea of the capacity of the different engines can be arrived at with a sufficient degree of accuracy. It is certain that in all three cases the engines are of high efficiency, and represent both in the selection of their proportions and in their general assembly a very high standard of locomotive design and construction fully representative of the latest British practice and worthy of maintaining the high reputation enjoyed by locomotive engineering designers in this country.

Railway....	Southern.	Southern.	Great Western.
Class	*King Arthur.*	*Lord Nelson.*	*Castle.*
	t. c. q.	t. c. q.	t. c. q.
Total weight engine	80 19 0	83 10 0	79 17 0
Adhesive weight ....:	60 0 0	61 19 0	58 17 0
Bogie weight, on	20 19 0	21 11 0	21 0 0
Total weight, engine and tender	138 10 0	140 4 0	126 11 0
Cylinders, number	2	4	4
,, diam.	$20\frac{1}{2}$ in.	$16\frac{1}{2}$ in.	16 in.
,, stroke	28 in.	26 in.	26 in.
Valves	Piston	Piston	Piston
Motion	Walschaert	Walschaert	Walschaert
Wheels—			
Coupled, diam.	6 ft. 7 in.	6 ft. 7 in.	6 ft. $8\frac{1}{4}$ in.
Bogie, diam.	3 ft. 7 in.	3 ft. 1 in.	3 ft. 2 in.
Boiler—.			
Largest diam. outside	5 ft. $5\frac{3}{4}$ in.	5 ft. 9 in.	5 ft. 9 in.
Barrel length	13 ft. 9 in.	13 ft. 9 in.	14 ft. 10 in.
Tubes, No. and diam.	169—2 in.	173—2 in.	201—2 in.
Flues, No. and diam.	24—$5\frac{1}{4}$ in.	27—$5\frac{1}{4}$ in.	14—$5\frac{1}{4}$ in.
Length between tubeplates	14 ft. 2 in.	14 ft. 2in.	15 ft. $2\frac{7}{16}$ in. (over tubes).
Heating surfaces—			
Tubes	1,252 sq. ft.	1,282 sq. ft.	} 1,885·62 sq. ft.
Flues	464 ,,	513 ,,	
Firebox	162 ,,	194 ,,	163·76 ,,
Total evaporation	1,878 ,,	1,989 ,,	2,049·38 ,,
Superheater	337 ,,	376 ,,	262·62 ,,
Combined	2,215 ,,	2,365 ,,	2,312·00 ,,
Grate area	30·0 ,,	33·0 ,,	30·28 ,,
Steam pressure	200 lb.sq. in.	200 lb. sq. in.	225 lb. sq. in.
Tender—			
Water capacity	5,000 gallons	5,000 gallons	4,000 gallons
Fuel	5 tons	6 tons .	6 tons

ESTIMATED DATA.

Rated tractive force at 85 per cent. of boiler pressure	25,320 lb.	33,500 lb.	31, 626 lb.
Weight on drivers ÷ tractive force	4·7	4·14	4·25
Engine weight ÷ combined heating surface	81·8	79·0	77·3
Boiler proportions.			
Rated tractive force ÷ combined heating surface	11·4	14·17	13·7
R.T.F. × drivers, diam. ÷ combined heating surface	900	1,120	1,100
Combined heating surface ÷ grate area	73·8	71·7	76·4
Firebox heating surface per cent. of combined heating surface	7·35	8·20	7·06
Firebox surface ÷ grate area	5·4	5·88	5·4
Superheater surface per cent. of combined heating surface	15·2	15·9	11·3

Appendix 2

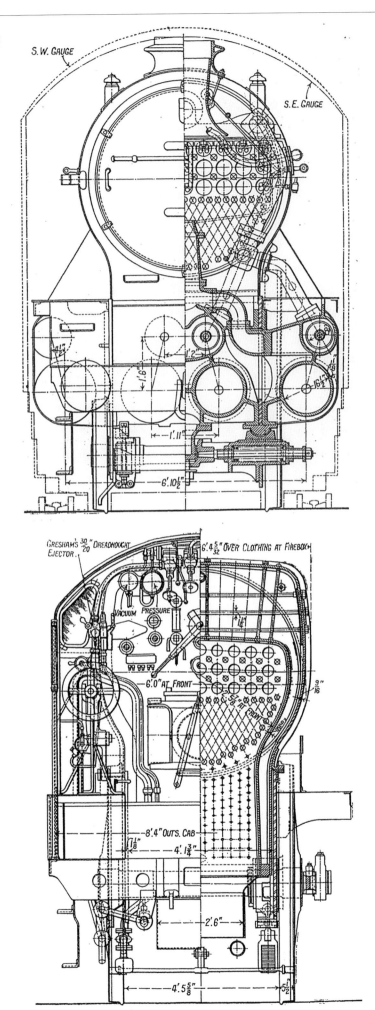

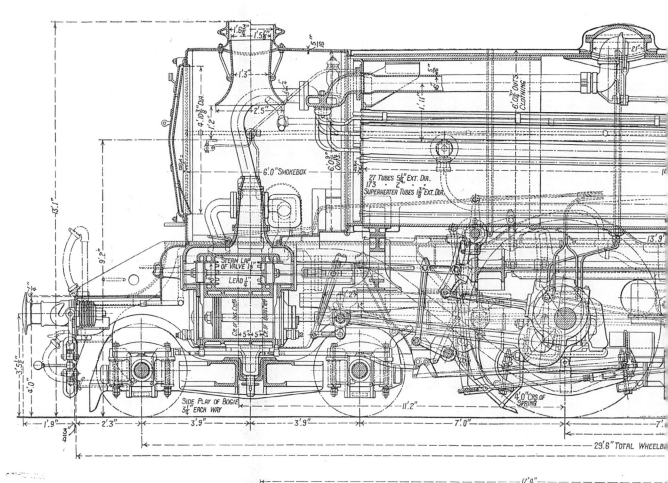

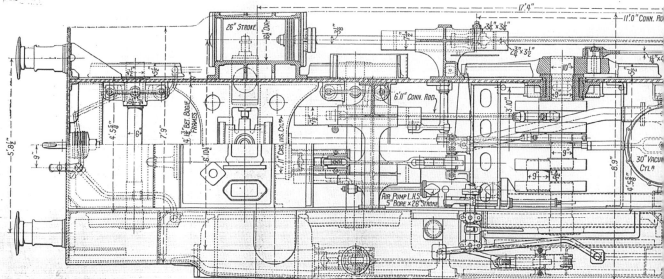

SECTIONAL ELEVATION, PLAN, PART END VIEWS AND PART SECTIONS OF FOUR-CYLIN

Mr. R. E. L. Maunsell, C.B.E., C

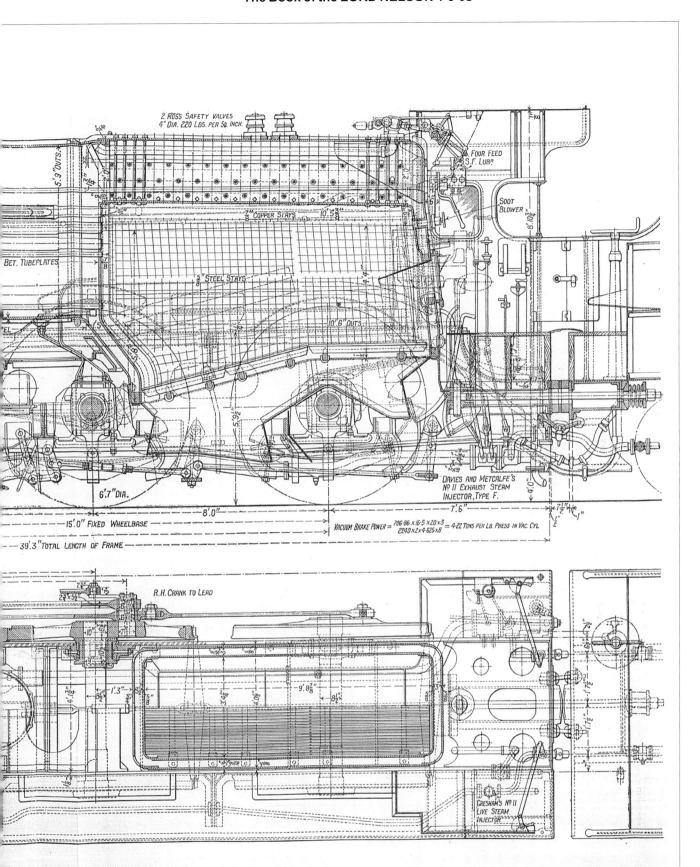

2 ROSS SAFETY VALVES
4" DIA. 220 LBS. PER SQ. INCH.

FOUR FEED
S.F. LUBR

SOOT BLOWER

COPPER STAYS

STEEL STAYS

BET. TUBEPLATES

10' 6" OUTS

DAVIES AND METCALFE'S
Nº II EXHAUST STEAM
INJECTOR, TYPE F.

6.7" DIA.

8'.0"

7'.6"

15'.0" FIXED WHEELBASE

VACUUM BRAKE POWER = $\dfrac{706 \cdot 86 \times 16 \cdot 5 \times 20 \times 3}{2240 \times 2 \times 4 \cdot 625 \times 8}$ = 4·22 TONS PER LB. PRESS IN VAC. CYL.

39'.3" TOTAL LENGTH OF FRAME

R.H. CRANK TO LEAD

9' 8⅞"

GRESHAM'S Nº II
LIVE STEAM
INJECTOR

ER 4-6-0 TYPE EXPRESS PASSENGER LOCOMOTIVE, "LORD NELSON," SOUTHERN RAILWAY

ief Mechanical Engineer.

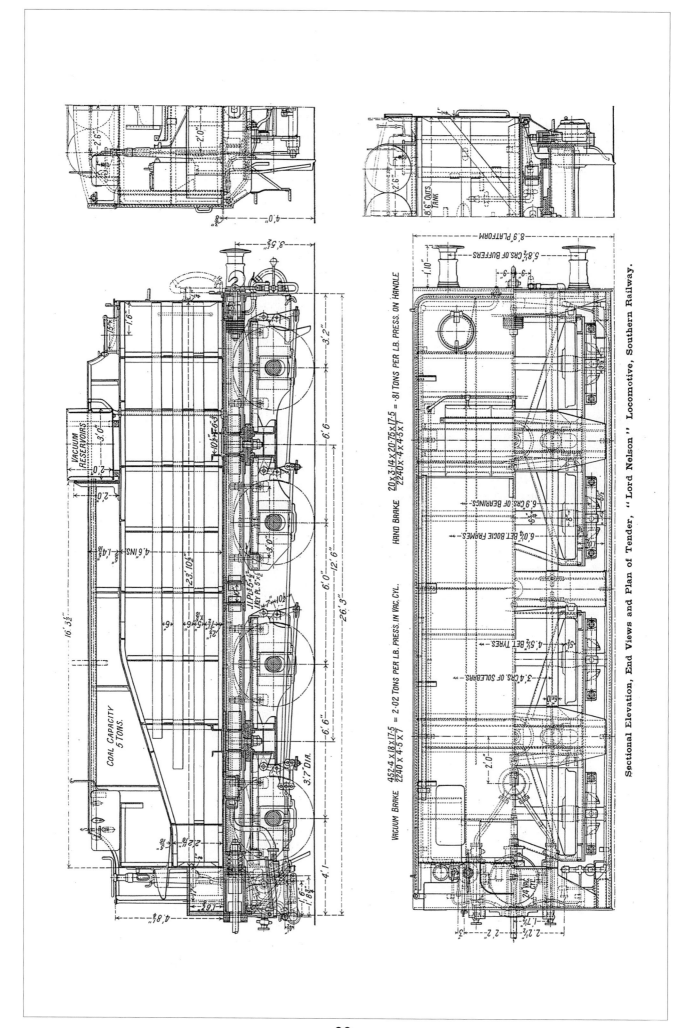

Sectional Elevation, End Views and Plan of Tender, "Lord Nelson" Locomotive, Southern Railway.

Appendix 3 Signed by Sir Herbert Walker, General Manager.

SOUTHERN RAILWAY MAGAZINE.

GENERAL MANAGER'S OFFICE,

WATERLOO STATION, S.E.1.

October, 1926.

NEW SOUTHERN RAILWAY EXPRESS ENGINE.

In order to meet the ever-increasing weight of our fast passenger traffic, a new express engine, No. E.850, the "Lord Nelson", has been built at Eastleigh, and is now ready for service.

The "Lord Nelson" is the most powerful passenger locomotive in the British Isles, and is the first of a series to be known as the "Nelson" Class. The design is by Mr. R. E. L. Maunsell, the Chief Mechanical Engineer. The engine has been built to haul trains of 500 tons at an average speed of 55 miles an hour, our heaviest trains at present weighing from 425 to 450 tons. The overall dimensions of the "Lord Nelson" will enable it to run on any main line of the Southern system.

The new engine is slightly heavier and considerably larger than the famous "King Arthur" Class, and is of four-cylinder design as opposed to the "King Arthur's" two, is superheated, and has six coupled driving wheels each 6 ft. 7 in. in diameter. The weight of the engine is 83 tons 10 cwt., and 140 tons 4 cwt. with the tender, while the "tractive effort" (at 85 per cent. of the boiler pressure the figure by which the power may be judged) is 14.96 tons, the highest in the country. The British engine with the highest tractive effort on the same basis hitherto has been the Great Western Railway's "Castle" Class (14.12 tons); while that of the L.N.E.R. "Pacific" is 13.32 tons, and that of the "King Arthur" is 11.31 tons.

A remarkable feature of the new design is that concerning the number of impulses per revolution of the wheels. Usually this is four, but in experiments with an older four-cylinder engine, by which the number of impulses was increased to eight per revolution, a considerable increase in efficiency was obtained; this arrangement has been embodied in the new "Lord Nelson".

Walschaert valve gear for both inside and outside cylinders is employed, and the revolving and reciprocating parts have been made extremely light by the use of a special high-tensile steel. The boiler pressure is 220 lb. to the square inch, 20 lb. more than that of the "King Arthur" Class. The cab has side windows of glass, and tip-up seats for the driver and fireman, and the tender is similar to those of the "King Arthurs" except that it has straight flat sides with no overhanging coping.

When other engines of the "Nelson" Class are built they will be named after the following Sea-Kings :—

"Lord St. Vincent".	"Howard of Effingham".
"Lord Howe".	"Sir Francis Drake".
"Lord Rodney".	"Sir Walter Raleigh".
"Lord Hood".	"Sir Richard Grenville".
"Lord Hawke".	"Martin Frobisher".

This new class in no way renders the "King Arthurs" obsolete; on the contrary, a further batch is about to be constructed.

H. A. Walker.

'Not another bloody Nelson!'
Coming next: The Book of the Schools 4-4-0s...

The Transport Treasury